MAKING SENSE OF THE

ICU

JOURNEY

A Family Guide to Critical Care

Thomas Ardiles M.D.

Making Sense of the ICU Journey
© 2023 by Thomas Ardiles M.D.

For inquiries about bulk orders please email:
3J12medicalresources@gmail.com

ISBN 979-8-86639-312-1

"This book should be handed out as suggested reading to all families upon admission of their loved one to the unit! Dr. Ardiles clearly, but completely, describes so much of what it is that we do every day in the ICU, and helps to paint a beginning road map for how families can navigate this difficult path. His expertise, understanding, and compassion shine through these words. Having a loved one in the ICU is hard enough, but with this book you can begin to decode some of the mystery and fear of the unknown in the ICU. Highly recommended for all families, and even nursing students and medical students!"

Mandy Osborne, ICU Nurse/Flight Nurse

"This book is very simple and allows those who are not medical professionals to understand the ICU, which is why it is perfect for patients' families. I believe it will be an excellent resource for families as well as new ICU Nurses, because it allows them to get an idea of the 'overall' picture."

Carlos Lara, ICU Nurse

"This book is absolutely beautiful and a tribute to the ICU, like a love letter to the steadfast work we do saving lives. It is set up as a useful tool for families and patients, with areas for notes at the bottom of the page and an index of terms and keywords for quick reference. Though it's geared toward families, even new graduate Nurses would benefit from the depth and breadth of the topics in this book. It really is a great resource for anyone who works in the Intensive Care Unit."

Lindsey Medeiros, ICU Nurse/ECMO Coordinator

"When a loved one ends up very sick and in the ICU, it can be quite overwhelming. Most people don't have any idea what to expect. In this book Dr Ardiles does an excellent job of simply laying out the information that is important to know and that isn't always explained eloquently or covered fully in the moment. It covers much of what a family would want to know and helps to guide them in their questions for the staff and providers. Not knowing what to expect, what to ask, or even what to worry about can add to the overwhelm and this book is a must-read for anyone who may be facing this situation with a loved one. It should be available in every ICU for families to read, but would be a great resource to new staff in the ICU as well. So much of what goes on the ICU is covered very succinctly here while at the same time setting realistic expectations of what we can and can't do. I would never wish for anyone to have to read this book, but for those who do, this is an excellent resource to help during a very difficult time."

Eddie Watson, ICU Nurse & ICU Advantage YouTube Channel, founder

"While it is true that all of the information in this book is technically available on the internet, I think patients (and their families) will prefer this book because the information Dr. Ardiles presents is personal and comforting."

Dr. Shamsid-Deen, M.D., ICU Doctor

"Family members often feel overwhelmed and frustrated when their loved one is in the ICU. This book helps provide family members with an easy-to-follow framework to ask

the correct and necessary questions about their loved one's progress during their stay in a critical care setting. This book is easy to read and follow and it explains the more common devices and treatments encountered in the critical care setting. It is an excellent guide that will help loved ones familiarize themselves with what our patients are experiencing and better understand the daily events that can occur while their loved one is critically ill."

Dr. Quiroga, M.D., ICU Doctor

"This book is an easy-to-read and concise reference for families navigating the complexities of caring for their loved ones in the ICU. It translates complicated medical jargon into clear and digestible information for families and patients. As a physician myself, I would recommend this book for anyone who has family in the ICU and needs a simple yet detailed roadmap on how to navigate the ICU."

Dr. Aashiv Bharij, D.O. Internal Medicine/Hospitalist

"When our family was suddenly thrust into the foreign and uncertain world of the ICU, Dr. Ardiles compassionately and confidently coached us through the experience. Dr. Ardiles' years of expertise coupled with his love of helping people is clearly evident throughout this book as he makes the ICU easier to navigate by offering practical advice and insights, clear explanations, and invaluable tips. This is an exceptional resource to help you ask the right questions and work in cooperation with the medical team as you all help your loved one."

Lisa H., wife of ICU patient

"As a bedside nurse who has worked in the Medical and Cardiac ICU for 43 years, I feel this book will be an amazing gift for the families to read. I was blessed to work with Dr. Ardiles for many years and this book communicates the compassion he shows at the bedside. I benefited from reading it and I believe other ICU personnel will find it helpful as well. We all need to step back at times and remember how much information families are trying to process. It gives clear explanations that will help the families and lighten the communication load on the ICU team as well. Thank you, Dr. Ardiles, for writing this book."

Tami Bernstein, ICU Nurse, Medical and Cardiac ICU

CONTENTS

INTRODUCTION

If you are reading this, most likely someone you love is in the Intensive Care Unit (ICU). **This can be a very uncertain and difficult time and this book is especially designed to help you and your family navigate the ins and outs of your journey.** Since ICU patients are so very sick, the ICU Team almost always interacts with the families more than with the patients. *Understanding the way the ICU works, how the teams are structured and how to approach problems or situations that arise, will provide a map for you to follow and help you find your way.*

This book is born out of my experience of over 15 years of caring for patients and families in high acuity ICUs. My desire is that it helps you get a clear picture of YOUR very important role in the ICU and also lifts some of the weight off your shoulders as to what is not your role (but rather the role of the ICU team). I hope it also builds confidence that the ICU Team shares your family's desire to do what is best for your loved one.

I am deeply indebted to my nurses, my colleagues and the many, many ICU families with whom I have walked through these "intensive" years, for their feedback and support in writing this book...and for making it better.

The book is designed to allow you to take notes at the bottom of the page so, if a thought comes to mind as you read, please write it down! In my family we always say that you can tell how good a book is by how much it's been written in.

Lastly, I want to thank my family for standing by me through these years, and particularly my very patient wife who was "on call" when I was on call, waking up when I was called and not once complaining.

DISCLAIMER

This book is written with the use of my knowledge and experience as an ICU physician. It is not intended to replace medical advice. You should always talk with the Medical Team when you have questions. In many cases, I am expressing my opinions gathered from having seen and experienced many conversations with families, nurses and other medical professionals.

Since this book is directed to the community, I tried to keep the scientific references to a minimum. The intention is to help families understand how the ICU works and to have a better grasp of the situation while there.

This book refers specifically to ICU care within the United States. That said, I am certain that while the teams and availability of equipment may differ slightly in other countries, the concepts that relate to the patients still apply.

CHAPTER 1

Monday morning:

(A fictional story about Luke, Paul and Gary...3 patients with the same condition but different outcomes.)

On a typically busy morning in the ER, 3 patients come in, all have stomach pain and fever, and are getting sicker by the hour. The Emergency Room team quickly diagnoses them all with acute appendicitis requiring immediate surgery. Thankfully, 3 teams of surgeons are standing by and take them to surgery as soon as they are ready. The surgeons do a great job and all 3 patients receive the same great care, but they eventually get sicker during surgery and end up being transferred to the ICU.

The first patient, Luke, is 24 and an athlete. He has no medical problems and just participated in the Iron Man competition. Unfortunately, he thought he had food poisoning and didn't come to the hospital right away so that by the time the surgeons take him to surgery, his appendix has perforated, and his blood pressure drops during the operation. The Anesthesiologist gives him fluids, quickly realizes the infection is spreading and transfers Luke to the ICU for medications to help with his blood pressure drop (due to septic shock), and the necessary antibiotics. Though his kidneys are initially affected, he wakes up from surgery without further complications and recovers quickly. He transfers to the floor after 2 days in the ICU and goes home after 5 days with no problems.

· · · · · ·

Paul is 70 and has been struggling with Diabetes, High Blood pressure and being overweight for years. His family says he can barely walk one block without getting out of breath. His Diabetes has affected his kidneys and he has chronic kidney failure. During surgery they find his appendix is also perforated and his blood pressure drops, but in his case, the Anesthesiologist notices he is not making urine and that his blood is more acidic, so he feels it is best to keep Paul on the Ventilator and transfer him still intubated to the ICU. Here, the ICU Team can take care of his blood pressure due to septic shock, give him his antibiotics, and try to help him come off the ventilator.

Unfortunately, Paul has weak kidneys and, with the infection, they fail. He will need hemodialysis for some time. After the infection is better, and with the dialysis machine helping to remove the extra fluid, the ICU Team feels he can come off the ventilator. He is very weak and the Physical Therapy team feels that he would do better going to a Rehabilitation Facility. He stays in rehab for 2 months and then is able to go home.

Unfortunately, Paul's kidneys do not recover and he will be on dialysis 3 times a week for the rest of his life.

. . . . .

The last patient, Gary, is 50 years old. At 40, he developed a brain tumor that was very aggressive. After the brain tumor was removed, Gary did not recover well and could no longer care for himself. He can recognize his wife, but cannot carry on a conversation. A couple of years ago, he had a feeding tube placed since he was choking with his food. He has not been able to walk for years and has been struggling with multiple bladder infections. The last infection showed bacteria resistant to antibiotics. Because of his inability to communicate and his chronic constipation, he is not brought to the hospital very promptly and has a perforated appendix. The surgeons do their part removing the appendix and cleaning the effects of the perforation, but he is much sicker than our other 2 patients. His blood pressure isn't responding to the medications, the antibiotics don't seem to be working and his kidneys have stopped working. He comes to the ICU on a respirator. The ICU Team evaluates him and realizes that all his organs are failing. His liver is failing, his lungs are now inflamed and he is bleeding everywhere because he has lost the ability to clot. Sadly, he continues to decline.

His wife realizes that if Gary could see all that is going on, and that his chances of recovering are minimal, he wouldn't want to prolong his life under these circumstances. The family agrees to let nature take its course and Gary passes away peacefully, surrounded by his family.

My reason for telling you about Luke, Paul and Gary is that 3 people with the same condition can fare very differently in the ICU. Some differences can depend on the quality of the ICU care, of course, but much depends on the ability of the patient to heal.

CHAPTER 2

Let's get a General Idea

An ICU (or Intensive Care Unit) is an area in a hospital where patients can receive specialized care, that is sometimes called Intensive Care or Critical Care. This type of care cannot be given in any other part of the hospital. The ICU takes care of the sickest patients and provides a location where the ICU Team can quickly check on patients and immediately react to any change. *(For example: A Neurosurgical ICU is a unit where patients are monitored after brain surgery. Any quick change can be a sign of complication. Most of the time, patients that have brain surgery do well, but an ICU that is specifically geared to recognizing these particular problems is the best place for these patients to be.)*

How does a patient get to the ICU?

Patients arrive at the ICU in several different ways:

1). From the Medical Ward, also called "the floor" (For example: A patient with an infection gets sicker and organs start failing.)

2). From the Emergency Room (This could be a patient who has had a cardiac arrest or some similar and serious emergency.)

3). Following Surgery (Some complex surgeries such as Open Heart Surgery or Neurosurgery require care in the ICU afterward. Other complex surgery patients are monitored in the ICU afterwards at the discretion of the surgeon.)

4). Some patients arrive at the ICU as transfers from other hospitals.

Why does a patient need to be in the ICU?

The main reason is that the patient is really sick or can get very sick, or he is recovering from a high risk surgery. The care of this patient cannot be done in any other part of the hospital for one of the following reasons:

1). **Specialized Equipment.** Some patients need certain equipment that can only be used in the ICU, such as a Mechanical Ventilator (sometimes called a Respirator or "the Vent") or an ECMO machine. (See Chapter 5 for more detail.)

2). Device Monitoring. Certain devices, such as an Arterial line or a Balloon Pump for the heart, can only be monitored in the ICU. Sometimes the patient needs certain drains to be placed and cared for in highly sensitive places in the body, such as the heart or the brain, and these require very careful handling. (See Chapter 5 for more detail.)

3). Complex Medication use. Some patients need medications that must be increased and decreased ("titrated") as the patient responds to them. Other medications can have serious side effects, like when a "clot buster" is given to a stroke patient, and the patient needs to be watched carefully.

4). Blood test monitoring. Certain diseases, such as kidney failure, can present with dangerous blood work values (eg. high potassium), where quick intervention is needed. Other diseases can cause the Sodium levels in the blood to rise or sink to dangerous levels and these require careful correction. Complications of Diabetes, such as Diabetic Ketoacidosis, combine several of these factors since the patient needs both frequent blood checks and a carefully administered Insulin infusion.

5). General Monitoring. In other situations, patients in a medical ward sometimes just "do not look well", as in the case of a patient with Severe Pneumonia (a serious lung infection). These patients are evaluated by an ICU Team and, if appropriate, transferred to the ICU in case a Ventilator should be needed. If the patient recovers without the Ventilator, they will return to the regular floor. However, if they fail to improve or the stress on their bodies causes them to get worse, maybe even causing a Heart Attack, the ICU is the best place for them to receive prompt and expert help. Additionally, patients that have suffered severe Trauma and are at risk for bleeding also require ICU care.

Of course, this is not a complete list of reasons for patients to be in the ICU, but these common causes help explain what we mean when we say that the ICU is the place to administer specialized care, and where there are teams ready to respond to emergencies and react quickly in the care of the patient.

What does the ICU do for a patient?

This is a very important question to answer because it will help you as a family to understand what to expect.

The ICU can provide the necessary care for the patient: antibiotics for an infection, fluids when needed, machines to help the work of certain organs (like Dialysis to help the work of the kidneys or ECMO machines to help the heart and lungs). **These all help to do one thing: BUY TIME. And this**

is the most important thing the ICU is doing, buying time... that crucial time needed FOR THE PATIENT TO RESPOND AND GET BETTER.

*Imagine you decide to take tango lessons and then trip and fall and break your arm. You then find "the best Orthopedic surgeon in the world" on Google, fly to their office and get your arm treated by a fantastic surgeon. Now, all this surgeon can do is put your bone together (and probably do it exceptionally well); **he cannot make your bone grow back. YOUR BODY HAS TO HEAL ON ITS OWN** and its ability to do that is what will make all the difference.*

Unfortunately, debilitated people, older people, people with chronic illnesses or on certain medications that decrease the immune system, do not heal very well.

What can the ICU not do for a patient?

(If you have not read Chapter 1, you may want to stop and take a few minutes to read it now. It should partially help answer this question.)

While it may seem obvious, the ICU cannot change the patient's ability to heal or provide the strength the patient did not have to begin with. **A PATIENT CANNOT LEAVE THE ICU STRONGER THAN WHEN THEY CAME IN.**

Here are some examples of what that means:

1). THE ICU CAN'T IMPROVE YOUR ABILITY TO HEAL

As we all know, a young healthy person is better prepared to face the challenges in the ICU than a frail, elderly person with pre-existing illnesses. Whether patients end up in the ICU as a result of an accident or illness, factors such as age, and other chronic illnesses, such as Diabetes, High Blood Pressure, and a bad liver (liver cirrhosis), can all make it much harder for their bodies to heal. The "strength" of the patient also plays a role. A 60 year-old who runs 5 miles, 3 times a week, will do much better than a 60 year-old that cannot walk more than a block without tiring. The ICU cannot change that.

2). THE ICU CAN'T MAKE YOU STRONGER

I remember seeing a patient once who was not recovering well from Open Heart surgery. While most open heart surgery patients do very well and come off the ventilator within hours after surgery, this patient was not able to come off the Ventilator for days. After speaking with the family, it came to light that this patient had been severely depressed and completely inactive for months before the surgery. He would literally "sit on the couch all day doing nothing." Sadly, the surgeon did not know any of this, and these circumstances caused the patient to be unable to recover as quickly as most people.

By contrast, I remember placing a patient with a severe Flu infection on ECMO. He was in his 60s but very strong and physically active. He began doing exercises in his bed as soon as he was able. Even though his lungs were very sick, he had the energy and strength to overcome this just like a much younger person!

Remember, nobody leaves the ICU **stronger than they arrived.**

3). THE ICU CAN'T CHANGE THE FACT THAT SOME PEOPLE JUST CAN'T SURVIVE

It's good to mention that sometimes the decision to bring a patient to the ICU is made in a hurry. This is often the case when a patient is struggling to breathe. In this situation, the compassionate thing to do is immediately to help the patient be able to breathe, sometimes even with a ventilator. The history can then be obtained in greater detail once the patient is more comfortable. Sometimes the team realizes only then that the patient has actually been sick for years, has been on a ventilator

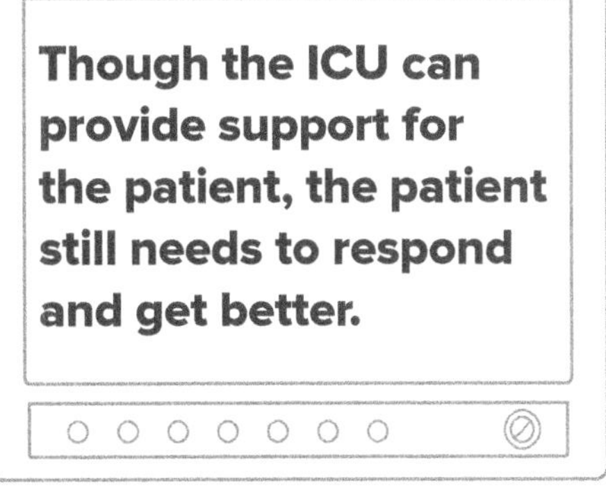

3 times this year already, and has been unable to eat without choking for weeks. Sadly, the chances of this type of patient doing well are small, and the ICU cannot change that.

The ICU Team does not always have the time to fully evaluate a patient's health before they arrive, and patients are admitted even when their health has been declining for years. In these cases, a patient comes to the ICU with very little chance to survive.

The following is a visual representation of the relationship between the patient and ICU care using the examples from Chapter 1.

A desirable relationship

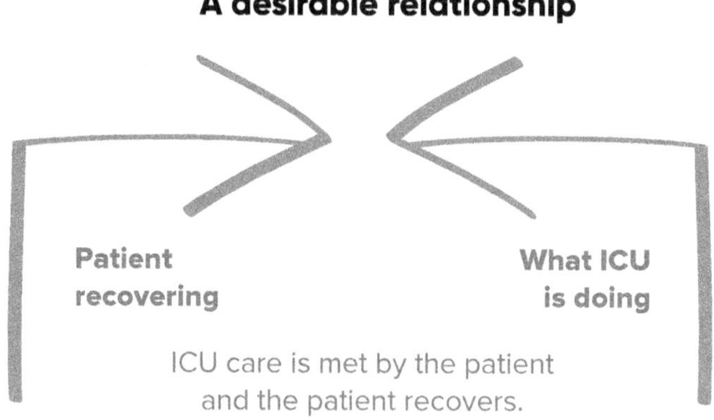

As in the case of Luke

**Patient
recovering fast**

**What ICU
is doing**

Patient is strong and recovers fast.

As in the case of Paul

**Patient Struggling
to recover**

**What ICU is
doing, patient not
responding fast**

ICU care is provided but patient is struggling
to recover and may not survive

As in the case of Gary

**Patient not
responding,
will probably die**

**What ICU is doing,
but patient does
not respond**

ICU care is provided, the patient never
responded to the point of recovery

Types of ICUs

There are several types of ICUs:

Medical: Treats medical illnesses such as severe pneumonia, serious heart attacks, sepsis, kidney failure, etc.

Surgical/Trauma: Is typically for care following a major Trauma or surgery. One key difference between these two is that the Trauma Surgeons that run the ICU are also trained Intensivists.

Cardiovascular/Cardiothoracic: Provides care following open heart surgery or other heart procedures.

Burn: Is for severe burns.

NeuroICU or Neurosurgical ICU: Typically for care following a Stroke, head bleeding or serious seizures. This is usually where the patients go after Neurosurgery.

Neonatal or Pediatric ICUs: These ICUs care for newborns and children under the age of 18. This book is intended for adult units only, since that is where I have worked.

Open or Closed ICUs: *Another way to classify the ICUs is as "open or closed" and whether there is an ICU Doctor (Intensivist) involved in the case at all times. We know that patients that have an ICU Doctor specifically assigned to them do better in the ICU. If you have doubts, ask if there is an ICU Doctor assigned to your case.*

CHAPTER 3

The ICU Team

A strong ICU is shaped by a great team working together in all areas to help patients get better. They do their part so the patients have the best chance to recover.

The following is a list of the team members and a description of what they do. (Some ICUs have smaller teams and do not have every one of these team members.)

Nurses

Teamwork in the ICU is exemplary. Senior ICU Nurses are always available to help more junior nurses. All an ICU Nurse needs to do is say out loud: "I need help in room 6", and you will see a number of nurses and other members of the ICU Team rush in to help.

ICU Nurse: I list the ICU Nurse first because this is the person with whom you will interact the most during your loved one's ICU stay. An ICU Nurse is a Registered Nurse who trains to become an ICU Nurse. Every hospital has its own training protocols, but each nurse is trained to ensure that they can work independently in the care of each patient.

The ICU Nurse will become familiar with the patient, will know the reason why the patient is in the ICU and the plan of care. They will know their medical history and will be the "eyes and ears" of the Medical Team, constantly using their assessment skills to see if things are going well and as expected, or if the patient is declining and a change of plan is needed.

The nurse will administer and manage all the medications and fluids and also chart all that information so that the team of doctors who are also keeping an eye on the patient can make decisions. The nurses provide valuable input for the patient's care, but it is ultimately up to the medical team to decide how to proceed. A nurse cannot give any medication without a written order from a member of the medical team who has a license to do so. If we need to transport a patient for an emergency CT scan, the nurses are trained and in charge of this complicated and sometimes risky trip to the scanner.

Get to know the ICU Nurses, they will be your best resource during your ICU stay. Sometimes even long term friendships can start in the ICU.

The nurse will also do the "less fancy" things like cleaning the patient after a bowel movement, and keeping the ICU bed clean and neat.

ICU Charge Nurse: There is always a charge nurse who is key to the function of the unit. The charge nurse assembles the Team for the next shift. If there is a sudden surge of patients in the ICU, the number of nurses needed will be higher than the previous shift. The Charge Nurse puts the team together, makes sure she has enough nurses and finds the nurses with the skills needed to take care of the patients. Charge nurses also can "float" (fill in where needed) and help the other nurses.

ICU Nurse Aids: Some hospitals provide Nurse Aids to help nurses with their tasks, whether turning the patients, keeping the rooms well stocked with supplies or being an extra pair of hands when needed.

TIP: Get to know your ICU Nurses! They are the backbone of patient care in the ICU.

The ICU Medical Team

The ICU Attending: This is the person ultimately in charge of the team, the **Intensivist.** Each patient is assigned one ICU attending. The ICU attendings typically work either the day or night shifts and are responsible for doing a "check out" to their incoming partner. They usually work a few days in a row and they typically have very long days.

The rest of the ICU Team will look different, depending on which type of hospital you are in.

In a teaching hospital, you will have **interns** and **residents** and sometimes **ICU fellows**. While these are all graduated doctors, they are still in training for their specialty and they all work under the ICU Attending.

While a resident may have the initial encounter with the patient during the day and may have an initial plan of care, the final plan of care is decided in rounds with the whole ICU team, under the leadership of the Attending.

In non-teaching hospitals, there will not be any residents. You will likely see the ICU attending or a mid-level provider that helps them, either a **Nurse Practitioner** or a **Physician's Assistant** who has been trained to care for ICU patients. Even though the teams are different, the ICU attending is always responsible for all final decisions.

Note: *The above situations apply to Medical ICUs. Of course, as we have discussed earlier in this chapter, there are several types of ICUs. In some, particularly in specialized Surgical Units like Neurosurgical ICU or Cardiothoracic ICU, many of the decisions come from the patient's* **Surgeon** *in coordination with the ICU Intensivist. The Trauma ICUs are unique in these situations, since the* **Trauma Surgeons** *are also trained Intensivists, in this case the Trauma Surgeon is also the ICU attending.*

Ancillary Staff

Respiratory Therapists: The recent COVID pandemic showed us the importance of the Respiratory therapists. Not only are they key in providing care for patients on the ventilator, they also make sure the ventilator is operating at peak performance. Respiratory therapists are also familiar with other forms of oxygen support and breathing treatments. They help the patients when they struggle the most to breathe and teach them to use machines such as the BIPAP (that helps give them air). In addition, they have expertise in evaluating when a patient is ready to come off the ventilator and they work with the ICU Doctors doing the "weaning trials" to help make this determination. As an Intensivist, you quickly learn to value the opinion of a good respiratory therapist.

ICU pharmacist: These are registered pharmacists that chose to get additional training to work in the ICU. They are very familiar with all the guidelines and standard of care and help the team make the right medication decisions. They will know the patient's home medications and typically help the ICUs design their protocols so that every patient gets the standardized care they need. They are a very important set of eyes in the fluctuating condition of the ICU patient.

For example, sometimes an antibiotic dosing has to be adjusted if the kidneys begin to fail. In most hospitals, the pharmacist will be relied on to adjust the antibiotics dosing to the kidney function. They will always be vigilant and keep the medical team posted.

Additionally, ICU pharmacists help "narrow" the antibiotics when possible, so that the "big guns" are kept for the future, if needed.

Dietician/Nutritionist: The body needs food to live and this is no different for a patient in the ICU. Most patients that are on a respirator will get their food and all their nutrition in the form of Tube Feedings. It is the Dietician/Nutritionist who understands what is going on with the patient, evaluates how many calories they need, and determines the best way to administer these. (For further discussion on nutrition, see chapter 7, section 9)

Physical, Occupational and Speech Therapists: As mentioned before, being sick to the point of coming to the ICU is very hard on the human body. Most people just get weaker during their stay. As they are improving and seem to be out of imminent danger, it is a good idea to start them on some form of therapy. Sometimes, this can mean just moving the arms and legs so they don't get stiff from being in the same position for prolonged periods.

As the patient gets better, these three types of therapists work with them to get them stronger. They also evaluate the patient and, when needed, will recommend that the patient be transferred to a rehabilitation facility where they will be provided with the extra time and therapy needed before going home.

Social Worker and Case Manager: Being in the ICU is hard not only on the patient but also on the family. Social workers and Case managers are there to support the families. They understand issues with insurance and at times they are even able to get the patient further options. A Social Worker and Case Manager can also help to evaluate the choices available to the patient when they are ready to be discharged. Sometimes the ICU Team recommends the patient go to an Acute Care Rehabilitation hospital to continue care. It is the Case Manager who looks for the options available to the patients. They also help families fill out paperwork such as Family Medical Leave forms, etc. Additionally, they can provide clarity for families when it comes to knowing who the Surrogate Decision Maker is (the person that can decide for the patient) if the patient did not appoint anyone before becoming unable to do so. If you want to find a Social Worker or Case Manager, ask either the Unit

Clerk or your nurse to have them connect with you. There is always a person on call.

Chaplain: There is no doubt that Spiritual care is part of the support that both patients and family need. If this is something that you would consider, ask your nurse to connect you with a hospital chaplain or ask if circumstances allow for an individual of your own choosing to come to the hospital.

Unit clerk: Every ICU has a Unit coordinator who helps answer phones, fax documents, request and receive records and do clerical work, so the other members of the medical team can focus on caring for the patients.

Housekeepers: These are the individuals who work hard to keep the units clean. They are in charge of preparing the rooms for the arrival of the next patient. It was very touching to me to work in the pandemic with our housekeepers, they are not paid much but they care about what they are doing. They are a crucial part of a well-run ICU. Most of the time they go unnoticed. Every time you get the chance, be sure to thank them for what they do!

To summarize, hospitals and ICUs may have different types of teams, but they all cover the same functions.

Tip: *Some ICUs keep a white board in the rooms that lists the ICU Team. These help keep families informed from day to day. The board lists the names of the Nurse, Medical Team, Respiratory Therapist, etc. working that day. Some write the goals for the day on the Board as well. Make use of the Board if you have it!*

CHAPTER 4

The ICU Journey

It will help so much if you can get a grasp on the BIG PICTURE early in the ICU journey.

The BIG PICTURE is made up of these 4 key pieces:

1). What made the patient sick: is it an infection, an accident, a heart attack?

2). What are the complications that are happening at the same time or may develop later?

3). How is the patient responding to treatment?

4). What was the patient's ability to heal before all this happened?

Keeping these interlocking pieces in mind will help you focus on the BIG PICTURE.

The 3 Phases of the ICU journey:

A. The Critical Period

B. The Recovery and Waiting Period

C. The Exit Plan Period

Obviously, these do not apply to every single ICU patient. A patient recovering in the ICU after an Open Heart surgery may only be in critical condition for a few hours and then quickly recover and be ready to leave the ICU the next day. Sometimes a patient has very high blood pressure because of forgetting to take their pills; they need just a few hours of IV medications while the pills start to work and they never are "critical". They only need to be in the ICU due to receiving a very potent medication. And sometimes, this critical period is very intense and short and the patient does not survive beyond it.

Unfortunately, setbacks can happen and while a patient is in recovery or even working on the exit plan, a new complication sometimes develops and the patient goes back to another critical period, moving backward rather than forward.

Typically however, an ICU patient will progress from The Critical Period through the Recovery and Waiting Period to the Exit Plan Period.

A). The Critical Period

The Critical Period is when patients first come into the ICU and their life is in danger. The ICU Team will work using its knowledge and skills in providing what the patient needs to get better. The situation may seem chaotic to a worried family, but a well-run ICU will immediately do several things: start treatments, obtain more information (through blood work, x-rays or Ultrasounds), administer medications and fluids, give oxygen, call consultants (if an emergency surgery or procedure is needed) and try to keep the family informed. Very commonly, the ICU Team will perform procedures that are needed to help the patient such as an intubation (to connect the patient to the ventilator), or inserting a central line or an arterial line. The team will try to get consent from the families, but in an emergency situation the procedures needed will be carried out in order to save the patient's life.

Very frequently, the ICU Team has to take care of multiple life threatening problems facing the patient simultaneously and it may not be clear right away which one is the main problem.

For example, a person that has been sick for days before coming to the hospital may be very dehydrated (and need fluids) but they may also need antibiotics (because the team suspects an infection) and maybe their Diabetes is out-of-control because they are so sick and they need an Insulin infusion. All of these things have to be taken care of **at the same time.**

In most cases, once the most pressing issues are improving and the treatments are in place, then the ICU Team can begin to get a better understanding of what the real issue is. Sometimes things are so complicated that this still may not be clear.

A lot of times the ICU Team is not able to talk to the patient and get a history of what happened or where they hurt etc. They must put things together while at the same time working to get the patient out of an immediately life threatening situation.

During these hours, families will see many people coming in and out of the room, "all hands on deck", until the situation is under control. When the patient is finally left with his own ICU Nurse, this is usually an indicator that things are starting to calm down.

The room may look very different at the end of these hours. There will likely be more equipment than at first and there may even be a lot of trash and supplies floating around since the care of the patient is always the priority. The team will come around and tidy the room as soon as it is feasible.

Sometimes the ICU Team will ask a family member to step out of the room for a time. This may be due to the fact that some things may be disturbing to watch and some people panic or even pass out and this pulls crucial team members away from being able to focus on the patient. But this may also be necessary because of a sterile procedure (to protect the patient) or when using equipment with radiation such as an X-ray machine (to protect the family member).

When requested, it is best for the family to go to the waiting room and be available to the team when they are called.

TIPS:

- ***Make sure it is clear who the decision maker is:*** This person does not necessarily need to be the contact person, as in the case of an elderly wife who is the surrogate decision maker. She may prefer to have her children keep her informed. In this case, the children would get the updates but it is the patient's wife who is the decision maker. A Social worker can help you think through these details.

  You should know: It is not unusual for the ICU Team to ask for the patient's Living Will or Medical Power of Attorney documents at this time. Please do not panic, this is a routine request!

- ***Be patient:*** The ICU Team wants to keep you informed, but they have to care both for your loved one and other patients in the ICU that may not be doing well.

- ***Be available:*** There are times when a person's life is in danger and the team wants to be able to let you know right away if things take a turn for the worse. If you cannot be available in person, provide a phone number where the contact person can be reached and also the number of a backup person, if possible.

- ***If quite some time goes by and you have not received an update:*** Kindly ask the unit clerk or the patient's nurse if the family can get an update.

- ***Try to always focus on the "BIG PICTURE"*** *(see page 39):* If the patient had a stroke and the brain is swelling to the point that it puts their life in danger, don't worry too much about their Diabetes, the ICU Team will handle that.

- ***Don't forget WHO the patient is:*** Is your loved one young and strong with no medical problems or a debilitated person that is not very strong and has a lot of medical problems? A weaker person has less energy to fight with than a strong one.

- ***Ask if you should call family in when things seem critical:*** While none of us can predict the future, sometimes things look very bad. My recommendation is to always communicate with family (especially those that are not close by) and let them decide when it is time for them to come. Loved ones rarely get angry if they come ready to say goodbye and are surprised with the news that the patient is getting better. It is more peaceful for all when the family is kept informed and they can decide for themselves.

- ***Try to get some rest:*** One of my ICU colleagues used to say to the families: "This is not a sprinting race; this is a marathon." I agree. Your loved one will probably need you more when they recover than they do right now.

- ***If you need something, ask:*** There are always Social Workers available at the hospital to help you if you are from out-of-town and don't have a place to stay. They usually know of hotels that provide discounts. Some hospitals have funds to help out-of-town families. Don't be afraid to ask for a snack if you did not eat. Someone in the ICU will gladly help you.

B). The Recovery and Waiting Period

After the scary Critical Period comes the "Recovery and Waiting Period." This is the time where the patient may not be in an immediately life threatening state, but is still critically ill.

You will see that these are more "normal" days in the ICU. Most interactions will be with the ICU Nurse and Respiratory Therapist and with the Medical Staff. Don't forget the "BIG PICTURE" (see page 39) and ask if things are getting better. "Baby steps" forward are always good, sometimes not getting worse is good because the baby steps may be too small to see and may become more obvious in a couple of days. Ask if there are new complications or if things have not changed. **Remember, all the ICU Team can do is give the body the conditions to heal. The body has to do the healing.**

As part of the BIG PICTURE, it is OK to ask your nurse what the **plan for the day** is and at the end of the day, see if the patient made progress or not. It is impossible to predict who will make progress and who will not, but if the patient is not making progress over several days and they should be, the team will start looking at possible reasons why. *For example, we think that after a heart attack the heart should be able to start pumping on its own with no help from medication, but if the nurses can't wean the medications off as intended, we have to look at why that is happening.* Sometimes it is just that the patient needs more time, sometimes there could be another reason.

Some places use **ICU Checklists** to make sure the important things are reviewed and discussed. Checklists are particularly key for complex patients since the most pressing issues tend to get the attention and the less crucial things can be forgotten. By using checklists consistently, the team can rely on them to ensure that all the important details for the patient are being cared for. *Feel free to ask your ICU Nurse if the ICU uses a checklist.*

As you see the days go by, you will also notice that the ICU Team may allow the patient to be a bit more "awake" (if medically appropriate) and the patient may be able to interact with family for a few minutes at a time.

You may notice some physical changes in your loved one. The most common one would be that they will look Swollen. There is an old ICU saying that says "you have to swell to get well."

While there is some truth to that, too much **Swelling** can have complications and it is the responsibility of the ICU Team to manage that. There are many reasons for the swelling to happen, including the large amount of fluids that sometimes patients need when they are unstable and the fact that a sick patient tends to "retain fluid" and swell up. Ask your nurse and your medical team if the swelling is concerning, they can give you an idea if they need to intervene and help the patient get rid of some fluids. (That can be done with medications if the kidneys are working well, or with the help of a dialysis machine if they are not.)

While the patient is still in the ICU, recovery can have setbacks. Try to remember the marathon analogy, **rest and pace yourself** as much as possible and try to be patient so that you will have the strength to step up when you are needed.

A word about the "stable" ICU patient:

Unfortunately, I have seen a lot of confusion in families due to the inaccurate use of the term "stable" by hospital personnel. A stable patient is by definition a patient that is out-of-danger and in a regular ward. This cannot be truly said about any ICU patient. While the intent is to comfort you that there are not any drastic, life-threatening changes going on, a patient in the ICU is always in survival mode.

Let me tell you a story to try to illustrate what I mean. Imagine you are driving your car along a winding road on a rainy day. Suddenly, your car slides out-of-control and is only kept from plummeting off a cliff by the broken guard rail. You grab your phone and dial 911. You are not falling, but man, if you try to leave your car or move too much, you might. You would not tell the 911 operator that you are "stable." You would beg for help as quickly as possible.

Kindly ask for clarification if someone says your loved one is "stable." Try to direct your questions toward the main problem and how the patient is responding to what is being done.

I am always careful not to say that someone on life support is stable. "Stable" means that if the equipment were removed from the room, the patient would be fine. We all know that isn't true. Sometimes the patient is "unchanged" from yesterday, and remains on the same amount of support as before. That is much different from being truly "stable" but that is what the person is trying to communicate with that expression. You must keep in mind that while they remain in the ICU, your loved one is still seriously ill.

TIPS:

- ***Don't call too early in the shift:*** Most ICUs work in 12 hour shifts, the daytime shift runs 7am-7pm. You will likely be asked not to call too early in the shift to allow time for the nurses to assess the patients and get started on the plan for the day.

- ***Try to be brief on the phone:*** The nurses are super busy and they typically have 2 patients to care for. (Though sometimes they get only 1 patient if the patient is very sick.) Multiple calls also delay what they need to do to take care of the patient.

- ***Have ONE family member be the point of contact:*** It is VERY hard for the ICU Team to be answering phone calls from multiple family members. The risk of misinformation is also higher since there are multiple conversations going on. *If possible, it is best to have ONE person or sometimes two people that can be a 1st and 2nd point of contact with the family.* They are the ones getting the updates and communicating with the rest of the family.

- ***Get some updates directly from the Medical staff:*** These updates may not be given on a daily basis but the Medical Staff can provide more information than a nurse normally can. While no one wants to give inaccurate information, people communicate things differently and the doctor, being responsible for the plan of care, can answer your questions directly.

C) The Exit Plan Period

As the patient continues to recover, there will be plans made for leaving the ICU.

There are two types of recovery: a normal or even fast recovery and a long term, slow recovery. There is, of course, not a set amount of time for any recovery, but it does help to remember that recovery times vary.

Remember our young, athletic, Iron Man competitor named Luke (from Chapter 1) who has a perforated appendix. He will likely recover faster than Paul who is elderly, has Diabetes, is overweight and also very inactive. It is important to keep this in mind.

If the patient is following the normal recovery, you will see that fewer of the things that can only be done in the ICU are being done for the patient. The ventilator is removed, the patient is awake from sedation, the blood pressure is holding on its own, the patient can eat and start physical and other forms of therapy. After the ICU sees these signs of "stability", and these signs are maintained for a reasonable period of time, it is likely that this patient will be transferred to the regular floor.

If the patient is debilitated and it is clear that a quick or normal recovery is not an option, the medical team will likely inform the family of this and connect them with a Case Manager to look at the different options they have available to them.

This is usually the case for patients who **struggle to come off a ventilator.** Sometimes they just need more time and more therapy. The medical team may recommend a tracheostomy (the inserting of a temporary more comfortable breathing tube and also likely a feeding tube) and that the patient be evaluated for transfer to a facility that specializes in weaning patients off the ventilator and in providing therapy. The family is always presented with the options (though these are sometimes limited by what the insurance is willing to pay), and a joint decision is made by family members and the medical team.

Please note, this is not a bad outcome. It does NOT mean the patient won't recover. It just means the patient needs more time. Of course, things can change and patients from these facilities occasionally come back to the hospital, but most of them do very well. Again, this is the time to remember WHO

Get to know all the therapists that are working with your loved one. Their input about just the right placement after discharge can be very valuable.

the patient is. If they started their ICU journey very weak, they are only weaker now and their recovery will be slow and may not be free of new problems.

CHAPTER 5

I. THE EQUIPMENT

The ICU Room, the ICU Bed, the ICU Monitor, Infusion Pumps, the Ventilator, the Dialysis Machine, ECMO, and the Balloon Pump/Impella Device are the most common equipment you will see in an ICU. Here is a brief description of the function of each.

a). The ICU Room:

There is nothing particularly special about an ICU room, but you will see by contrast to other areas of the hospital that they can be in "pods" to allow for better visibility of all the patients. They are also designed to allow equipment to come in and out, and they will always be a single bed room (The only time in my life that I saw two patients in one

ICU room was during the Covid-19 pandemic.) The rooms will also have hook ups in the walls for oxygen, suction and compressed air for the ICU equipment. Some rooms will have a negative pressure feature that keeps airborne infections from spreading.

b). *The ICU Bed:*

The COVID pandemic caused a bit of confusion here. At the peak of the pandemic, we kept hearing, "We are short of ICU beds." That did not refer to the actual beds, but rather to the facilities and the medical team necessary to care for the patient in the bed. Beds can be moved from other floors, but the staff and equipment to care for the patients is limited.

The beds in the ICU are especially designed to facilitate the care of the patient. They have handrails for safety and an awake patient can be allowed to control the bed position. Typically, the bed is kept elevated at a 30 degree angle to decrease the risk of aspiration of oral secretions that can eventually lead to pneumonia. This is very important. Some beds have the ability to "vibrate" to help the patients manage secretions. Some beds have specialized functions that under special circumstances may help the patients recover more quickly (like a bed that can turn the patients or has a particularly soft surface to allow wounds to heal).

If a patient is very heavy, the team usually orders a Bariatric bed. This bed is not only larger, but has extra features to help in the care of the patient, such as a special mattress that helps prevent bed sores and makes movement of the patient easier.

c). *The ICU Monitor:*

Placed up high and to one side of the bed, the monitor looks like a TV but is actually where the patient's vital signs are shown. It typically shows the Heart rate (how fast the heart is beating) and the EKG/ECG tracing (showing the rhythm of the heart beat, whether regular or irregular), the Blood pressure (either checked by the cuff or continuously checked by an arterial line), and the number of breaths per minute. Most monitors will also show the percentage of Oxygen saturation, together with an undulating (wavy) blue line. Some monitors may show the last temperature checked and can be programmed to show information from other equipment, such as sophisticated Cardiac output machines or other pressure monitors.

All the ICU monitors are connected to **Central Monitoring,** meaning that the results are shown at a nurses' station at ALL times. If an alarm goes off in any room, the whole Unit is informed and they can act on it.

A word on the monitors and their interpretation. While the information on the monitors is key for the ICU Team caring for the patient, please bear in mind that the interpretation is complex and can lead to confusion and unnecessary anxiety in family members trying to understand it.

For example, you may be able to see that a patient's heart is going at a very normal pace of 80 beats per minute, but the medical team knows from the patient's illness that it really should be more like 120. Because of their training, they know this is "inappropriately normal."

The Medical team also knows, for instance, that a "good oxygen saturation," such as 95%, also depends on how much oxygen is given to the patient. If the patient is connected to a ventilator, it will additionally tell the Team how much the ventilator is pushing those sick lungs. Shooting for a "great saturation of 99%," could potentially and irreparably hurt those lungs. Sometimes less is more and it takes the team's expertise to decide on the strategy they will need.

It is also good to point out that the monitors just "show" information. They do not provide any treatment to the patient.

d). *The Infusion Pumps:*

The infusion pumps are medium-sized boxes with buttons and a small screen found on either side of the bed.

These are connected to the fluids and medication lines that are given to the patient.

The job of the pump is to deliver the medication at the intended rate and within the programmed safeguards. The pumps are programmed for each medication each time they are placed and deliver the amount programmed at the speed programmed. The nurses are all trained in managing the pumps and they are the ones running the pumps, not the doctors. The pump's alarm will sound if the medication isn't delivered as expected or if there is a blockage on the IV line (like when an awake patient bends the arm where his IV catheter is). It has safeguards to keep it from delivering air into a patient. If you see an empty bag and a pump alarm goes off, don't be "alarmed," the patient is not in danger and the nurses have been notified and will take care of it.

> When someone is really sick, you may see as many as **10** or more **infusion pumps** at the bedside. **As the patient gets better, you will see fewer and fewer infusion pumps.** This is usually an indicator that the patient is getting better.

e). *The Ventilator:*

The function of the Ventilator or "Vent" is to help the patient's own lungs to help the patient breathe. Sometimes those lungs are very sick.

The Vent not only provides Oxygen, it also "inflates" the lungs "for" the patient so the body can use the oxygen it needs to heal. One important thing to remember is that our natural breathing "lets the air in" when we take a breath. The Ventilator "inflates" the lungs the same way we inflate a balloon. This "unnatural" way of breathing is called Positive Pressure Ventilation, and while it buys time and allows the patient to recover, if it is not done very carefully it can cause severe lung damage. The ICU Doctors are specially trained in implementing what is called a "Lung Protective Ventilation," striving to minimize the potential damage this unnatural means of breathing can cause.

The sicker the lungs are, the harder the Ventilator has to push to inflate the lungs and the more careful the team has to be to avoid problems.

For a patient to come off the ventilator, the following things need to happen:

1). **The reason for the patient to be intubated has to improve.**

Is the patient's pneumonia (or whatever was the cause for the intubation) getting better? Or in the case of a heart attack patient, is the heart doing better? If the patient suffered a stroke and was in a coma, is the patient waking up?

2). The Ventilator has to be slowly reduced to "minimal" settings before the patient can be "weaned from" (transitioned off) the Ventilator.

The medical team is typically looking for Oxygen less than 50%, "Positive End Expiratory Pressure" or PEEP around 5 (the higher the PEEP, the sicker the patient) and, most importantly, a recovering patient.

3). The ICU's Ventilator Weaning Protocol has been met.

ICUs typically have protocols for removing patients from the ventilators. Typically, when the patient is ready, the nurse wakes up the patient and the Respiratory Therapist does a "Spontaneous Breathing Trial" or SBT. If the patient passes the SBT and is fully awake, the ICU Doctor will then decide if the tube can come out.

It is important to know that even if the patient looks great and all the indicators point to their readiness to come off the Vent, about 10-15% of patients will need to be re-intubated and placed back on the Ventilator. If this happens, the ICU Team then goes to work to find out why and draws up a plan to correct the problem.

f). The Dialysis Machine

Kidneys sometimes stop working and need help carrying out their important functions. Thankfully, there are dialysis machines that can help with some of the work the kidneys do. However, while they can "clean" the blood, they cannot replace ALL of the complex workings of the kidney.

There are 2 types of dialysis machines: the **"Conventional" Hemodialysis Machine** and the **"CRRT" (Continuous Renal Replacement Therapy) Machine** . While both do similar work, they have several differences:

- **CRRT Machines** require less blood flow through their circuit, therefore they work better with unstable patients and are typically managed by the same ICU Nurse that is caring for the patient. These machines run 24/7.

- **HD Machines** require higher blood flow out of the patient, and the patient has to be more stable to tolerate this. Typically, HD nurses will come to the ICU and "run" the patient for a few hours and either remove fluids or electrolytes, as directed by the kidney specialist.

Both machines need a large intravenous access to get the blood out of the patient to the machine. In some cases, the ICU Team has to place a **Temporary Dialysis Catheter** to facilitate this process. This has become a very routine procedure.

At times patients start with CRRT and then transition into regular HD when they can tolerate it better.

g). The Balloon Pump and Impella Device:

Both of these devices work to support the heart by augmenting the amount of blood or blood pressure as the heart pumps the blood out. While working in very different ways, both are designed to be placed temporarily until the heart recovers from what made it weak. For both, a large catheter connecting the machine to a large artery is usually placed in the leg to access the heart. A patient must be kept very still while the catheter is in place since sudden leg movements can be dangerous.

ICU Nurses know how to run these machines but they always work under the direction of the Cardiologist or Heart Surgeon, who typically decides when it is time to try the patient on a lower setting and when the patient is ready for the machines and connecting catheters to be removed.

In the case of some patients with heart problems AND circulation problems, the catheter placed in the artery that brings blood flow to the leg actually blocks the blood circulation in the leg. This forces the team to remove the catheter so the leg isn't injured through loss of circulation.

h). **The ECMO Machine:**

In extreme circumstances where the heart is not working well or the lungs are severely injured to such an extent that a lung protective strategy isn't possible (the lungs are too sick, making the ventilator "push too hard"), the ICU Team will call for an ECMO (**ExtraCorporeal Membrane Oxygenation**) evaluation. If the patient is a candidate, the ECMO team will place ECMO cannulas (plastic tubes) in the patient to take the blood out of the patient, run it through a pump and an oxygenator (that does the work of the lungs) and then send blood rich in oxygen back into the patient. This allows both the heart and the lungs to rest, while the body recovers. We always say that ECMO is a "bridge to something, not a destination", it could be a bridge to recovery, or a lung or heart transplant. But whatever its purpose, it is important to have an exit strategy because these therapies are complex and not free of complications.

This is of course a very simplified explanation. A patient on ECMO requires very specialized care outside the scope of this book.

It can be helpful to note when ECMO is being offered to your loved one, that a busier hospital with a higher number of ECMO patients should mean it also has a higher level of expertise in this area.

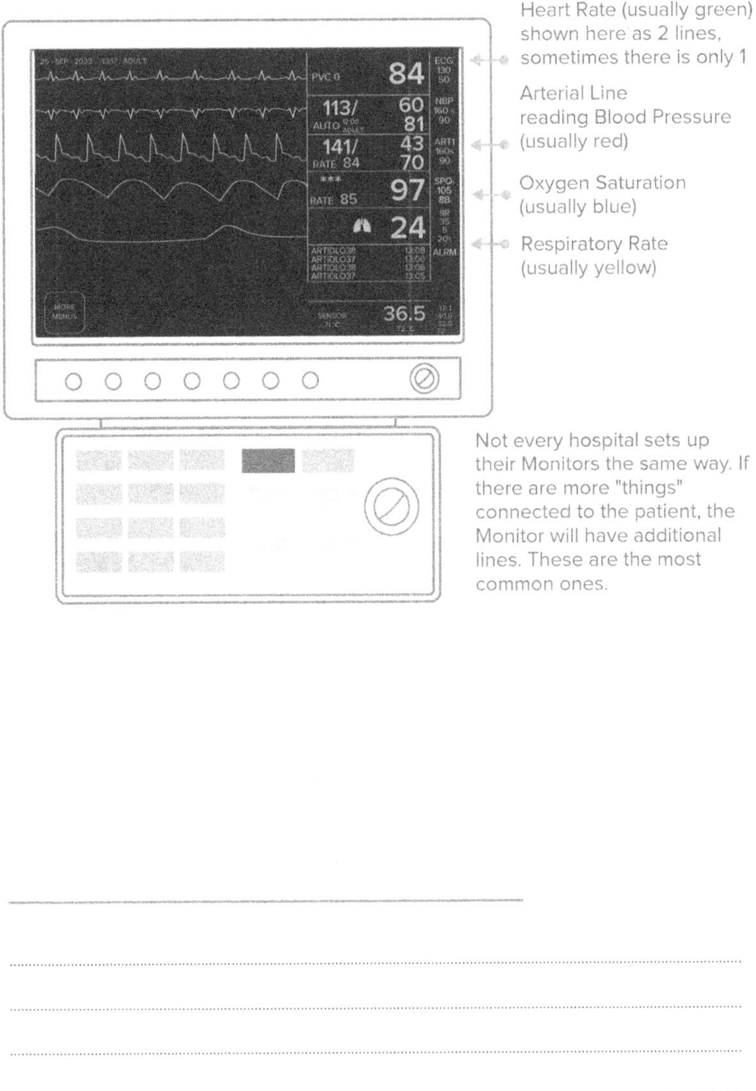

Heart Rate (usually green) shown here as 2 lines, sometimes there is only 1

Arterial Line reading Blood Pressure (usually red)

Oxygen Saturation (usually blue)

Respiratory Rate (usually yellow)

Not every hospital sets up their Monitors the same way. If there are more "things" connected to the patient, the Monitor will have additional lines. These are the most common ones.

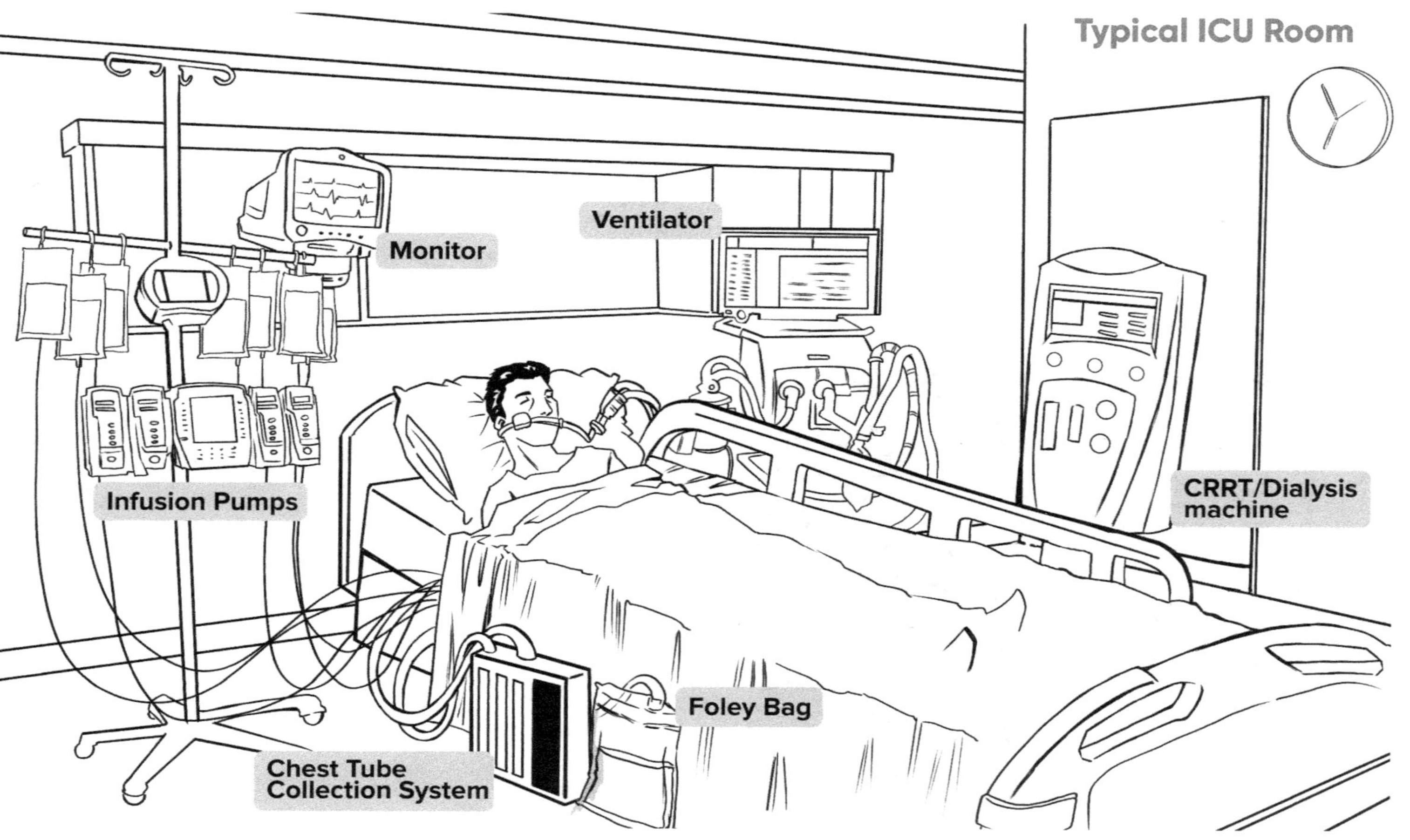

Typical ICU Room
Monitor
Ventilator
CRRT/Dialysis machine
Infusion Pumps
Foley Bag
Chest Tube Collection System

II. COMMON ICU (MEDICAL and NURSING) PROCEDURES

Procedures are general medical interventions that typically do not require an incision and are less invasive. There are several types of procedures. A procedure can be something as simple as starting an IV. This is a **Nursing Procedure** which, as its name implies, is carried out by the nurses. The placing of a Urinary Catheter, as described below, is another example of a Nursing Procedure.

Following each procedure, I have listed potential complications that can arise. These are not always related to the procedure but to the device or the presence of the device inside the body, as in the case of an infection. Not all complications are related to the procedure but "come along" with it. This includes loss of intended function as in, for example, the case of a drain that does not work because it was placed to drain blood that has now clotted and will no longer flow.

a). *Nursing Procedures:*

1). **Foley Catheter:** This is a Nursing Procedure in which a Urinary Catheter (a tube) is placed in the urethra (the tube that carries the urine out of our bodies). It helps the ICU Team measure the urine output (how much urine is made per hour), which is a sign of how the kidneys are working and is also helpful if there are concerns about obstructions. The Foley Catheter needs to be removed as soon as possible, since it is prone to infections. Sometimes it has to stay in for a bit because the patient may be sick for a longer period, making the Catheter necessary. Most seriously ill patients will have a Foley Catheter

Complications: rare and minimal from the placement, but can get infected or cause harm if accidentally misplaced or removed.

2). **Nasogastric (NG) or Feeding Tube placement:** This is a Nursing procedure, in which a tube is inserted into the stomach from the patient's nose. It can then be used to give both nutrition and medications.

Complications: rare and minimal. Minor nose bleeding, misplacement to the lungs (nurses check the placement initially and then we always follow up with an Xray to be sure)

TIP: Nurses are WAY better than the doctors at doing the Nursing Procedures, operating the Infusion Pumps and handling the sometimes stubborn ICU Beds and ICU Monitors.

b). *Medical Procedures*

These are only carried out by the Medical Team. These procedures, which require consent (if there is time), can carry more risk but can also save a patient's life. They should be explained by someone from the Medical Team who will also answer any questions you may have.

Complications can sometimes happen but they are NOT very common.

3). Central Line/Catheter Insertion: This is sometimes called a Triple Lumen (3 tubes-in-one) Catheter. (Catheter is another name for "small tube".) There are two main reasons why this is needed: 1. to have reliable IV access and 2. to place certain medications in a larger vein so there is very little risk of the medication blowing through a small broken vein.

The Central Line will be placed in a large vein either in the neck (internal jugular), groin (femoral vein) or under the clavicle (subclavian vein). This is done under sterile conditions and the team is trained in inserting the catheter and will usually use Ultrasound to guide placement. This is a very common procedure, the main risk is injury to the structures that are close to the vein, such as arteries or, rarely, the lung. The Medical Team can give you a better idea of what the procedure will look like. Once the Central Line is inserted, the nurses, or sometimes a dedicated IV team, will make sure the lines stay clean and that there are no signs of infection.

Complications: rare. Damage to adjacent structures, bleeding, infection or needing to replace the catheter.

4). **Hemodialysis Catheter/Line Insertion:** This tube is inserted in exactly the same way as the Central Line described above. The difference is that this tube is thicker so it is a little harder to place. Sometimes patients who need emergent dialysis do not clot very well and there can be some bleeding.

If the patient needs dialysis for a long period of time, this catheter will need to be changed for a more permanent one, called a "Tunneled" Catheter. This will usually be placed after the kidney doctor and the ICU Team determine that the patient will need more time to recover or will need permanent dialysis. This Tunneled Catheter is typically placed by the Interventional Radiology team and the patient needs to be stable enough to be transported to the Interventional Radiology suite.

Complications: rare. Damage to adjacent structures, bleeding, infection or needing to replace the catheter.

5). **Arterial Line Insertion:** An Arterial Line is needed when the blood pressure is too low or too high, since a blood pressure cuff is not very accurate under these conditions. In these situations, the medical team will recommend placing a Cannula (much like an IV) in an artery.

This gives beat to beat readings of the blood pressure, and it also gives the ability to draw blood without constantly poking the patient. Since the Cannula is inserted in an artery, there is a risk of bleeding, hematoma or injury to the artery, but these are rare. It is extremely rare to see any infection develop.

Complications: rare. Malfunction and needing to replace the line, bleeding with accidental removal.

6). **Intubation:** This is the procedure in which we place a "breathing tube," sometimes called an ET Tube (Endotracheal Tube), through the mouth, into the patient's lungs so we can connect the patient to the Ventilator. While well tolerated by someone who comes from home for an elective surgery, this procedure is much more delicate for someone who is sick in the ICU. Normally, the Medical Team will quickly sedate the patient and temporarily paralyze the muscles, so the tube can be placed safely. This sometimes takes away all the "adrenaline" the body was using to stay alive and the patient gets sicker. As you can imagine, when the lungs are sick, keeping the patient from breathing by paralyzing the muscles is not ideal. This can be a risky procedure and it is only done when absolutely necessary. The key is not to do it too late, when the intubation has become extremely hard to carry out but also not too early, when it's not yet necessary.

Complications: in the hands of an experienced person, placing the tube is usually not very complicated. It is what we are trained to do. However, the sedation, muscle relaxation and placement on a ventilator can cause the patient to crash due to drastic changes in the body.

7). **Bronchoscopy:** This is a procedure that is used to obtain deep sputum samples from a particular area of the lung, to localize a source of bleeding or remove a foreign object, etc. A small flexible tube with a camera and a light is usually introduced through the Endotracheal Tube, or ETT, (although it can be done in non-intubated patients) and directed by the doctor to the problem area. While it can cause coughing and some discomfort, it is in general a very safe procedure.

Complications: rare. Rare minor bleeding, transient drop of oxygen during the procedure but this is closely monitored.

8). **Chest Tube Insertion:** This is typically done when a lung collapses and there is a need to remove air from the chest that can "crush" the heart and make a person very sick. This tube is placed AROUND the lungs, not into the lungs, and can be used to remove fluid and/or air. There are two types of chest tubes: 1. Small bore, usually called Pigtails (because they curl like a pig tail) or 2. Regular or "Surgical" chest tubes (that look more like plastic tubes such as a small garden hose). Both have advantages and it will be the medical team's decision which type is needed. The main complications are bleeding and, very rarely, lung injury.

Complications: rare. Placement can be painful and cause some bleeding, they may malfunction and need replacement. In rare cases they are placed into the lung, causing injury.

9). **Swan Ganz Catheter Insertion:** This is a specialized catheter (sometimes referred to as a Pulmonary Artery Catheter) that is placed using access through a central line (described above). This catheter is placed from the vein, using a balloon to follow the blood flow from the right side of the heart to the Pulmonary artery. This is particularly useful in caring for patients with a failing heart, due to Heart Failure or Cardiogenic Shock. These catheters can sometimes be tricky to place. The Medical Team uses the waveforms in the monitors to know where to place them or sometimes the Cardiologist will place them in the Cath Lab under fluoroscopy (which is like a continuous X-ray). They are not very commonly used, except in the case of heart patients. The main complications are misplacement and sometimes the misinterpretation of the information the catheter provides.

Complications: rare. Misplacement, bleeding and misinterpretation of the data.

10). **Paracentesis**: Some patients build up fluid in the abdominal cavity (the stomach). Ninety percent of the time these are patients with a sick liver. Infections are common in this fluid, and the fluid build-up can make it difficult for a patient to breathe. The Medical Team uses Ultrasound to find where the fluid is and through Paracentesis, can remove a small amount to test for infection or a large amount to let the patient breathe better. Some patients with liver problems don't clot well after the procedure and bleeding can be a major problem. At other times, the puncture wound does not heal well and will leak fluid for a while. That said, in general, this is a low risk procedure.

Complications: rare. The most devastating is bleeding in a patient with liver disease who can't clot.

11). **Cardioversion:** Sometimes the heart's rhythm goes wild and a sick heart (or even a healthy heart) doesn't handle that well. Cardioversion delivers a shock to the heart to stop the abnormal rhythm so that the normal rhythm comes back. The extreme form of this procedure is needed when people's hearts stop all together due to a lethal form of an arrhythmia that needs Defibrillation. The intense shock from a defibrillator is designed to pull the patient back from death and restore the heart to its normal rhythm. This may be done as an emergency as sometimes there isn't time to call for permission.

Complications: in this case, the procedure is performed but the patient may not respond and may remain unstable.

12). **Drainage:** This is a general term used for removing fluid (that is usually infected) from a place where it has collected and should not be present. Depending on the location of the fluid, this procedure can be done at the bedside, but sometimes the fluid is in a delicate place and requires a specialized team from the Interventional Radiology Department. This team can use a CT scan to access the area of build up. If someone is sick from an area of fluid that is infected, antibiotics are rarely enough to take care of it and those collections usually need to be drained.

Complications: rare. Bleeding, misplacement or the catheter can stop draining and need replacement.

The list above contains only the most common procedures. There are other procedures done in specialized ICUs and your medical team is the best source of information as to the risks and benefits of each of these.

CHAPTER 6

A Typical Day in the ICU (what goes on Behind the Scenes)

Tips to connect with the ICU team

As its name implies, the ICU can be an intense place. It is truly a 24/7 operation with many things happening behind the scenes that you may not be aware of as you support your loved one. The following is a depiction of a typical day, and though hospitals have different ways of doing things, they will not deviate too much from what I will describe.

A TYPICAL DAY IN THE ICU
(What goes on Behind the Scenes)

Around 4 or 5 am: The ICU Nurse typically sends the "morning" or daily labs that allow us to check on the patient. These results are usually available in an hour or so and the nurses typically review them and call the doctors with any concerns. The ICU Medical Team is also mindful of the results arriving and will be keeping an eye out for the results. Some abnormal results will require immediate action by the night teams so the corrections are done by the time the day ICU Team arrives. If a Chest X ray is done, the abnormal findings are also addressed by the night team if they have time.

By 6 am: Most of the day Medical ICU Team has arrived and is getting ready for the day. They will talk to the night nurse briefly to make sure there were no major events in the night and will probably see the patient quickly. Then they will review the chart on a computer to see all that happened during the night. The day nurses are also arriving so they can start their turn, **typically by 7 am.** They obtain a report from the night nurse. The Medical Teams also obtain reports of what happened during the night from the night team. After the reports are done, the night teams can go home if they are done with their work, and care is now under the day teams. The day team will go in and examine the patient before rounds and will likely run into the consultants. Most consultants like to begin their day in the ICU, since these are the sickest patients in the hospital.

During the morning: The "big" event in the ICU is the rounds. In teaching hospitals, the Residents and Fellows will make sure they are prepared to present a patient to the attending during rounds each day. They are expected to know everything that has happened to the ICU patient, especially in the last 24 hours. **The team discusses the events, reviews all available test results and agrees on a plan for the day.**

For example, a plan for the day could be to give addition-al fluids to help address a low urine output, decide that the patient will only need antibiotics for 2 more days and put that stop date in the chart. Also decide that since the patient is recovering, it is time to start the protocol for weaning the patient off the Ventilator and call Physical Therapy to start some mobility exercises with the patient.

By the afternoon: After rounds are done, the work contin-ues with receiving new patients and transferring patients out of the ICU. A lot is happening behind the scenes: the nurses are always talking to the doctors and updating us about any-thing that can be of concern, whether it is a lab test or how the patient looks. The medical team is discussing the case with consultants, they are watching for the CT scan that was ordered, or waiting for a lab to come back. Additionally, there are multiple conversations with pharmacy, nutrition and case management. As you can see, though they may not be visi-ble to the family members, there are many, many necessary tasks being carried out on behalf of your loved one, as well as the rest of the patients assigned to the team.

By late afternoon: The day team is trying to make sure the plan for the day is completed and that there are no pend-ing tasks for the night team that can be accomplished during the day. While the ICU is open 24/7, in most hospitals the ICU teams are smaller at night.

Around 7 pm: Both doctors and nurses report to the night teams and the night teams assume control of the ICU.

Through the night: We all hope for a quiet night where the patient does not require unplanned tests or have to travel out of the ICU as in the case of an emergent CT scan. If they are able, nurses usually sponge bathe the patients at night. Of course, some urgent things do happen at night and if so, the night team will contact the consultants on call with questions and sometimes other doctors will come in to help with an unstable patient.

Before you know it, the morning labs are available again and the process starts all over with a new day.

Things to remember: the ICU should have the same capacity to operate day or night. The ICU Team is always available and while it may not be the normal day person if something happens at night, there is always someone covering for them. While most things happen during the day and we prefer to allow the patients to rest at night if possible, the night teams have the heavy burden of continuing to care for the patients during the night, allowing the day teams to rest and come back refreshed in the morning.

As you see, the teams are doing a lot behind the scenes that you may not be aware of as they work to stay on top of the patient's complex ICU care.

TIPS TO CONNECT WITH THE ICU TEAM:

Individuals who work and thrive in the ICU must have caring personalities and a special ability to work in a fast-paced and sometimes stressful environment. They enjoy working closely with their team and share a strong camaraderie.

The following are some of the ways you and your family can help foster a good working relationship with the individuals in your ICU team.

- **Get to know them:** The ICU staff understands the importance of working together and they will always welcome you as part of the team. When families get along with the ICU Team, the same nurses will usually "request" to work with the patient on their shifts and then get to know the patient better. The same can be said of the Respiratory Therapists and other staff. Get to know everyone by name, try to understand their function and show them your appreciation. Working during the pandemic has significantly decreased morale, a family that shows interest in getting to know the ICU Team can make a big difference.

- **Help them get to know the patient:** The ICU staff loves to hear about who your loved one is. If they are big music fans, maybe play their favorite music. If they are artists and it is possible, show off some of their art. You can put out family pictures and family notes to decorate the room (lightly). Most importantly, let the ICU Team know that you care for your loved one. Be available by phone, ask questions to make sure you understand the BIG PICTURE (if you need a refresher go back to page 39), and show an interest in what is going on. Visit your loved one and take turns with other family members, if they are available.

It affects the whole team when a patient is all alone and no one visits or calls for long periods of time, since the team truly cares about every patient. Of course, circumstances can be difficult such as when the only living relative is an elderly parent with transportation problems. However, a daily phone call to check on a loved one can still make a difference.

The ICU Team loves a family that cares for the patient.

- **Be mindful of the environment:** If you spend enough days in the ICU, especially when you are visiting frequently, you start getting a sense for what is going on around you. Often there will be someone one or two doors down the hall who may be "crashing" (in a crisis) and the ICU Team will deploy all of their attention to trying to save that patient. You will see people going in and out of that room, equipment being brought in, maybe a family in distress.

The reason to point this out is that this may not be the best time to ask questions that can wait until tomorrow or for a call later in the day.

The ICU Team will appreciate your awareness of what is happening and your consideration in helping them care for the sickest patient at that time, as they cared for your loved one.

- **Show your appreciation:** We all thrive when our hard work is appreciated and ICU Staff are no different. A simple thank you, a card that can be displayed in the Nurses' Lounge, a small sign in the patient's room...it doesn't need to cost much, you can be creative. Just let them know their efforts are appreciated.

I remember a family member that could make Origami figures out of Post It notes and would graciously offer them to us during rounds. Of course, ICU Teams are always hungry and if your gift is making cookies or buying donuts, they will always be welcome!

- **Come back to visit after you go home:** A few paragraphs above we discussed the importance of family presence in the ICU. A special bond is formed as the team fights to save a patient's life and finally sees them recover and leave the ICU. They know the families well and rejoice with them, especially in some of the more miraculous recoveries; but they rarely have a chance to truly meet the patients because they are so sick.

To see a patient walk into the ICU to visit brings great joy to the ICU Team and renews their motivation to continue caring for each patient, no matter how sick. It truly makes a difference.

AS A FAMILY MEMBER, WHAT IS MY JOB IN THE ICU?

This is a very important question. Sometimes families become consumed by endless internet searches seeking to gain the same level of knowledge and understanding as the ICU team. In my case, the training to be a Board Certified Intensivist took 14 years of intense work. In the last hospital where I worked, we had 3 nurses that had over 30 years of experience in the ICU each. This cannot be replaced by any number of hours navigating the internet.

I'd encourage you to realize that your primary job isn't to process all the information from the labs, monitors and equipment. Your primary job is one that no one else can do. Your loved one needs you to be their family...to be there with them, hold their hand, talk to them and inspire them with hope and a desire to keep going. I encourage you to consider yourself a part of the ICU team, but don't try to replace them.

But I like to be informed....

We all welcome that, we welcome that you care and that you want to understand what is going on with your loved one, but let's do that together as a team: use the ICU Team as your source for understanding what is going on, to get the BIG PICTURE. A Google search can't help you with that as it is not taking care of the patient and the answers you find will rarely apply exactly to your situation. And that is what you are looking for: good answers that apply specifically to your loved one's situation.

How can I make the best use of the Patient Portal?

Some hospitals give families access to the patient's data using a Portal. While they seek transparency and provide as much information to the families as they can, it is wise to use that information with caution. The decisions that are made for a patient are not only based on labs. They are based on the patient's diagnosis, clinical guidelines, the patient's response and the judgment of the medical team.

CHAPTER 7

Common Questions when it comes down to the Hard Decisions

The following are the most common situations that you may encounter, or wonder about, when you interact with the ICU Team. They may not all apply to you now, but it may be helpful to read them, as they may cover issues you will face later on.

1). ***I am not happy with the care my loved one is receiving. What can I do?***

When evaluating how you feel about the care your loved one is receiving, it may be helpful to separate the outcome (how the patient is doing) from the actual care the patient is getting.

The main source of problems is POOR communication, but it can also be the result of having the wrong expectations.

At times, Medical Teams fail to make sure the BIG PIC-TURE and the emerging problems are clear to the families. This can give rise to false or unrealistic expectations. For instance, a weak and debilitated patient surviving their ICU stay may seem to the family like the end of the battle when there is actually a long and difficult rehabilitation process ahead they had not anticipated and of which they were not well-informed. *Consider our examples from Chapter 1. Imagine if Gary's family had been told: "He is stable and we are giving him antibiotics for the infection.", while all of his organs are failing and he is not doing well. This would cause serious distrust and even anger when facing the reality of his imminent death.*

Often, there is disinformation if Medical Teams rely only on the Nursing Teams to communicate with the families. While the Nursing Teams are very knowledgeable about patient care and its complexity, it remains the responsibility of the Medical Team to communicate with the family and manage expectations. If you hear that the patient is "stable" and you know they are on some form of Life Support, be sure to ask further questions. I have seen this being a major source of confusion in the ICU. (See Chapter 4 for an explanation of why patients in the ICU are not "stable.")

Bear in mind that the ICU Team wants the family's experi-ence to be a good one and to be on good terms with them. **If you are not happy, it is advisable to think of the One or Two main reasons why you are not happy and bring them up to your bedside nurse first. He or she will know where to take**

it from there. They can connect with the Medical Team and advocate for you, if there is a need for more communication.

If the issue is with the hospital system, sometimes a Social Worker or Case Manager can be of help. They can also help with questions regarding discharge planning.

Whatever the situation, it is good to take a step back and consider your concerns, then communicate the one or two main issues and try to give the ICU Team an opportunity to fix them. As in any relationship, if those involved don't know what the problems are, they cannot work on fixing them.

2). *Why is my loved one not being fed?*

We have all been sick and we know that the sicker we are, the less we feel like eating. This is a natural reaction and is true of ICU patients as well. **The body can go a few days without food, using its reserves for energy. When the body is very sick, the gut "shuts down," partially to let the body use the blood and energy for the organs that need to fight. Food isn't a priority.** As the patient gets better, the Medical Team will slowly introduce nutrition. Most ICU patients need a temporary Feeding Tube through their noses into the stom-ach so they can slowly start receiving "Tube Feedings." They are fed specific formulas containing all the macronutrients and vitamins their body needs. Dieticians will help calculate the amount of "food" the patient needs to provide sufficient energy to help their bodies fight. Despite good nutrition, the body uses so much energy that most ICU patients lose a significant amount of weight and muscle. Don't let this overly alarm you, weight and muscle can be regained.

3). *What if I don't want my loved one discharged from the ICU yet?*

First of all, remember the reasons a patient needs to be kept in the ICU. Being transferred out to the regular floor is good news! Your loved one is better and no longer needs the ICU.

Normally you will have noticed that there are fewer Infusion Pumps, and other ICU equipment (such as the Ventilator, ECMO or Hemodialysis Machines) has also disappeared. Your loved one is looking better. These are indicators that the care the patient is receiving can be carried out in the same way on the Regular Floor.

It is natural to feel concerned that the care won't be the same on the Regular Floor, maybe because your loved one was originally transferred from the floor and you know there will be less "personalized" attention. But it is good to remember that this is a step closer to home and you can be sure that the Medical Team made this decision carefully.

The Medical Team makes the determination to move a patient to the Regular Floor based on the clinical condition of the patient. **If the patient improves enough that they can be cared for on the floor, that is a great start, but that is not the only consideration. For a patient to be moved out of the ICU, all of the consultants must be in agreement.**

In many hospitals, the Medical Team having a patient "bounce back" to the ICU is treated as a quality of care issue. It is never in their best interest to transfer an unstable patient to a Regular Floor.

4). *What is the purpose of a Tracheostomy and PEG (Feeding) Tubes?*

When a patient is not recovering quickly enough and needs to be given more time, a Tracheostomy or "Trach" can be key. A Tracheostomy is essentially a shorter breathing tube that still connects to the lungs but comes from the front of the neck (instead of continuing up through the throat and out of the mouth). **This is in general much more comfortable for the patients and they don't need to be sedated since they are no longer gagging on the breathing tube. (It also protects the voice box from damage.)** This is a huge benefit since the patient can now wake up and do all the needed therapy.

Feeding Tubes ("PEG tubes") are similarly beneficial. These are inserted directly into the stomach and are much more comfortable than a tube inserted through the nose.

Rather than feeling this is a defeat, it is good for the family to see these as helpful tools giving their loved one the time they need to recover. Unless otherwise stated, these are intended to be temporary while the lungs recover and the patient gains strength.

These are only considered permanent measures in some cases where the patient has brain damage due to low oxygen either from a cardiac arrest or a large stroke and they need help with suctioning secretions. Sometimes muscles fail and these patients need permanent help with breathing.

When you help make the decision and consider what the patient's own wishes would be, make sure to ask if the Medical Team feels this could be permanent, if they have not yet been clear on this point.

If any of these questions are concerning you, please ask the ICU team. Don't let your concerns build up to the point that they cause you anxiety.

There are advantages to placing a Trach early when we anticipate a slow recovery, since the Trach patient does not require that much sedation and can then participate in therapy. In most places, the Tracheosotomies and Feeding Tubes can be safely done at the bedside in the patient's own room. This depends on each hospital's capabilities.

5). *What is Long Term Rehabilitation or Acute Care Rehabilitation?*

This refers to further treatment the patient will need between leaving the ICU and being able to go home.

It is typically necessary in cases where the patient was too sick in the hospital to complete the required therapy to be able to go home. This may be the case of a young and initially strong patient who faces a severe situation such as multiple gunshot wounds that require multiple surgeries and therefore a lengthy recovery. Or it could be necessary for a patient with not much strength initially, who has developed a serious infection that won't let them recover fast enough.

The Rehabilitation Centers where the patients can go are usually coordinated with the Case Managers based on patient needs and availability of beds and are agreed on by the family/decision makers. **These centers specialize in providing the type of care needed for the patient (who usually requires a Trach and PEG for comfort) to come off the Ventilator and get stronger.**

PREPARING FOR THE DIFFICULT CONVERSATIONS:

6). *My loved one isn't getting better*

Ideally, every patient would be in the ICU for just a few days and have a quick and uneventful recovery. But the reality is that some people will not recover well, some will have a lot of complications and some may not recover at all. Being severely ill "drains" all the body has to give and if your loved one's sick and weak body did not have much to give, there will be little to draw from for recovery. However, even if they had a fairly strong body to begin with, a serious injury like a serious infection or severe trauma may simply be too much for the body to handle.

When do you know someone isn't getting better? **You can usually trust what you see.** There should be some signs of recovery, a perception of less worry in the ICU Team and "less action" in the patient room, as everyone waits for problems to improve. However, if there is some doubt, it is always acceptable to ask: Is John better? Are there any new problems? What should I worry about or what would be a good next **milestone** to watch for? Are there changes to the BIG PICTURE?

For example: if the patient is recovering from severe Pneumonia, is the Pneumonia better? Being on the Ventilator requires the patient to be kept comfortable with sedation and pain medication. Is John waking up OK or is he confused and agitated?

If you have been supporting your loved one and have an idea of the BIG PICTURE, you should have some sense of whether the main problems are improving or not. When in doubt, take a step back and ask the ICU Team, preferably someone from the Medical Team, to help you get some clarity.

Don't forget what we discussed earlier. The ICU Team and the care they provide are only part of the formula for success. The patients themselves HAVE TO RECOVER. Unfortunately, sometimes recovery takes a very long time or patients have set-backs such as a hospital-acquired infection. And sometimes recovery just isn't possible.

7). *What if we are coming to the End of Life?*

Sometimes the damage is too severe or the patient does not have the ability to recover. In these situations, organs often start to fail and no amount of support the ICU can provide is able to delay the inevitable coming of death.

While not infallible, the ICU Team has experience in realizing when things are beyond just having a bad day. When they communicate these observations, it is important to realize that there needs to be a conversation about End of Life.

The most important questions to answer in the End of Life conversation are:

- **What would the patient want? Did they ever express their wishes about this situation?**

- **What is the opinion of the medical team?**

- **Are all the decision-makers in agreement?**

These 3 pieces of information are crucial. Sometimes emotions get in the way and the family can forget what the patient would want if they could speak. I have personally told my family what my wishes are if we are ever in this situation, and would encourage everyone to do so.

What do you do if the patient did not express his/her wishes? In that case, my recommendation is that since the family knows the patient best, they should decide what the person would or wouldn't want.

Would Charlie sign up to be a sailor? "No way!", the family says; he hates the ocean, gets sea sick and can't swim. Would he choose camping over shopping at the mall? I am sure the answer to that will also be clear. The family that knows the person should have an idea of what the person would choose.

The job of the doctor's team is to provide their medical opinion. Please be mindful that they CAN'T PREDICT THE FUTURE. What they tell you is based on probabilities in cases with similar patients in the same situation. Exceptions and unexpected recoveries happen, but they can't predict that.

For example, when someone survives a Cardiac arrest, there is reason to be concerned about the damage their brain may have suffered, particularly if CPR was not given quickly or the patient did not respond quickly. Based on their experience, the ICU Team can tell you what they expect will happen next. But, as in the recent case of an NFL player who went into Cardiac arrest following a tremendous colli-sion with another player and received immediate attention, exceptions do happen. To everyone's amazement, within 72 hours he was extubated and calling his worried teammates. In this situation, we had an extremely fit athlete that got im-mediate qualified help, so both the ability to heal *and the right care were present.*

That said, End of Life conversations do need to occur. As you go through this tough time, it is good to remember that everyone involved is working toward what is best for the patient. It is especially crucial to keep in mind what he or she would have wanted had they had the chance to express their wishes. And don't forget that situations do change, and while a person may wish to fight when complete recovery is possible, their wishes may be different if some permanent disability is a strong possibility. *Remember Paul in Chapter 1? What if he had told his family in his sound mind that he WOULD NEVER want to have Hemodialysis, even if it was temporary?* That sort of background impacts your decisions.

8). How to understand the CODE STATUS

While there are some minor variations in code policies from hospital to hospital, the CODE STATUS is very similar.

- **FULL CODE:**

This status is for the patients who stand every chance of getting better. The Team will continue fighting with everything they have. Every reasonable effort will be made to save their lives.

- **Considerations for aggressive care**:

A rapidly declining patient is at risk of their heart stopping at any time. There will be a discussion regarding bringing the patient back, should this happen. As you think of this and make the decision for the patient, please always consider what the patient would say if they could speak for themselves.

A notion of the "BIG PICTURE" is very important here: is this the culmination of a decline that has been going on for days making the chances of survival poor? Or is this a new problem that may have a solution?

- **DNR (Do Not Resuscitate)**

It is important to know that saying "no" to CPR and requesting a DNR (Do Not Resuscitate) order does not mean that the team will stop caring for the patient or that anything will change. It only means that in the event of a Cardiac Arrest (where the heart stops), the team will allow nature to take its course.

- **DNI (Do Not Intubate)**

Sometimes patients draw the line at needing to be on the Ventilator and they choose not to take that treatment option. It is hard to separate that from a full DNR, since low oxygen will inevitably lead a heart to stop. When a heart stops, doing "partial treatment" (like compressions without placing a person on a Ventilator) does not work. Ask for your hospital's policy and check with your medical team what the best options are.

- **"No Escalation of Care"**

In some cases, it is a good idea for families to decide with the Medical Team that there will be "No Escalation of Care." This means that the team will not add any more care treatments, such as starting Hemodialysis or taking the patient to surgery, since it is felt by all that this will be "too much."

When we realize that the patient is not getting better, sometimes the right thing to do is STOP. The family and ICU Team are united in helping the patient get better and, when the patient cannot get better, their job becomes one of compassionate care, refusing to prolong the patient's agony.

- **CODE BLUE:**

"Code Blue" is the term used to notify the Code Blue team that a patient is in Cardiac Arrest. Cardiac Arrest means that the heart has stopped and the patient has died. At this point, in any hospital, Advanced Cardiac Life Support (ACLS) is started, this means Chest Compressions (CPR) with the intention to bring the patient back. First, the team that finds the patient immediately starts CPR (Chest Compressions). Next, a "Code Blue" is called overhead and the Code Team will come to the bedside to assist. Typically, once the Code Team arrives they take over the code. Code Teams can come from the Emergency Department or sometimes from the ICU.

Chest Compressions have to be strong enough to externally pump the blood and try to get it all the way to the brain and other organs. This can be hard if the patient is big or very sick.

Contrary to what is usually seen in TV shows or movies, a sick person in the hospital typically does not do that well after CPR. There are several reasons for this. First, they are sick and the sickness most likely has gotten to the point in which the body can't cope any more and the heart stops. Second, the patient may have a very sick heart, and no amount of CPR will fix that. Lastly, it does not take very long for a person to suffer serious problems from lack of oxygen. When oxygen is withheld, all the organs fail.

Unfortunately, as the main purpose is to externally pump the blood from the heart to the organs, injuries happen and broken ribs are not unusual. It is probably safe to assume just by nature of the effort necessary to bring a person back, that there will be a lot of pain in the chest after the compressions.

- **Withdrawal of Care:**

This is the commonly used term, however, one of my mentors taught me to call it "Removal of Support", because we never truly stop caring for the patient. Removal of support is the decision that can be taken when you know the patient would have never agreed to what is being done to keep them alive. If you are the decision maker, be outspoken with the Medical Team. It may be something reversible and there may be room for negotiation, but don't forget, what the patient would have wanted matters the most.

If you do opt to remove the support, I always advise to turn off the monitors in the room, so you can be with your loved one and not be distracted by the screens. The Medical Team is looking at them outside the room and they will continue to make sure the patient is comfortable. They won't let them suffer as they take their last breaths.

9). *When is it time to have an End of Life conversation?*

When the Medical Team can see signs that a Cardiac Arrest is imminent, they will start the conversation with the family regarding what should be done when/if the arrest happens. In this conversation, it is key to establish the following:

- *Is this the end of the dying process?* If so, is it necessary to submit the patient to the suffering of painful chest compressions when the outcome cannot change?

- *Is this something reversible and worth trying to pull the patient through?* I once took care of a patient who was young and had a healthy heart, but had a drug problem and intentionally inhaled a solvent that made his heart go into very serious arrhythmias. He went into Cardiac Arrest all through the night, but we did CPR again and again knowing that this was temporary and he had every chance of surviving. Eventually, he did recover.

Always ask yourself: "What would my loved one say IF they had a chance to be present in these difficult conversations?"

10). Will my loved one be ok after CPR?

Like any medical treatment, what happens after CPR depends on both the circumstances (a patient found quickly and receiving good CPR right away) and the ability of the patient to heal.

While all organs fail, the brain is especially susceptible to lack of oxygen. It only takes a few minutes for a brain to suffer permanent damage. The longer the CPR has to be done, the higher the chances of brain damage. Taking a long time to wake up after CPR also contributes to the chances of having brain damage.

Damage to the brain can have serious effects. This can range from being in a coma or in a "vegetal" state, to not "being the same person" anymore. Family members have to be able to decide: is this what our loved one would want?

11). I have to Keep Going, right?

After the patient has been in the ICU for a while, let's say ten days to two weeks, the Medical Team will have an idea of where things are going. They are either on the road to recovery, they are getting worse, or there just isn't much progress. *(Remember the arrow graphics in Chapter 2.)*

Sometimes keeping going is the right thing to do. Sometimes, we have to ask ourselves: What are we putting the patient through? Would he/she want this? If the answer is no, you have options.

Often, families don't know they can ask for advice and that they have options. If your loved one is a disabled 95 year old, offering Hemodialysis may be an option but that doesn't mean it is the right thing to do. At the same time, Hemodialysis is a great option for a younger person whose kidneys shut down due to a temporary cause.

Always ask your ICU Team. You don't have to keep going if it does not feel right and you feel the patient would not have chosen that option.

12). If we let him go, aren't we responsible for his death?

This is a common burden families feel when coming to decisions at the end of life.

If your loved one is struggling with cancer that is not responding to treatment and develops a serious infection because chemo knocked down their immune system, it is an option to consider that they might not want to continue aggressive care. The BIG PICTURE here is a patient with advanced cancer and low defenses trying to fight an infection with poor ability to heal.

If you think in your mind that your loved one would say, "This is enough, I don't want to continue anymore, please stop." and you express this to the ICU Team, your ICU Team will support you (as long as it is medically appropriate) because it is a reasonable option, given the circumstances of how the patient is doing. The KEY point in this example is: It is not YOU who is deciding if your loved one lives or dies, it is the CANCER that is taking their life. Your job is to honor your loved one's wishes and care for them when they no longer have the strength to speak up for themselves.

13). WHO decides? What if the whole family isn't ready?

This is a common question when someone is very sick in the ICU and cannot speak for themselves. In these cases, the decision is made by the SURROGATE Decision Maker or the patient's designated Medical Power of Attorney. If the patient planned ahead, they already asked a person to make decisions in case they became disabled. In the case of a living spouse, they are the default person.

Every state has slightly different definitions as to the Surrogate Decision Maker. You can clarify this with the Case Manager, if you aren't sure. **Typically the order is the spouse (sometimes only if legally married), adult children, other relatives, and close friends.** Please check with your Case Manager to see what rules apply to your situation.

Sometimes, there is a large family and it is hard for all of the family members to agree on what is best to do. There are different expectations or previous bad experiences in the ICU and everyone seems to be on a different page. **In these situations, it is often helpful to request a meeting with the Medical Team so they can answer any questions the family may have.**

Another reason to meet with the Medical Team is to get their advice. Though sometimes they fail to do so, it is my opinion that the Medical Team should provide guidance to the families. They should be able to say, "If I were in your shoes and this was my wife/mother/father/brother/son, etc, this is what I would do, for these reasons." I have repeatedly told my residents that when we take our cars to the mechanic, we always expect advice about what to do. Why would we not expect advice when dealing with a serious situation in the ICU?

Try to find out what is at the root of the disagreement within the family. Often they don't trust the medical system or they had a bad experience or they just need more time to process and see the patient before they can accept reality. However, it is important to set a SPECIFIC PERIOD of TIME to wait, because the longer you wait, the more uncomfortable the patient is and the more time we could be going against his/her wishes.

Considering that we all want what is best for the patient, we should have a reasonable timeline of days rather than weeks.

It is worth the effort to try to come to a peaceful solution as a family in order to preserve family unity so you can grieve together and celebrate the life of your loved one.

14). Should I consider Hospice?

Enrolling a patient in Hospice is sometimes the best thing to do. There is a lot of confusion about what Hospice is and what it can do for a patient. Sometimes people think Hospice is a place where people are simply sent to die. That is not the case.

Hospice care comes into play once modern medicine has nothing left to offer the patient; when the patient or the family choose to prioritize comfort over efforts to prolong life. This means, for instance, that the patient with advanced Cancer that has not responded to any Chemotherapy or Radiation, will no longer try to get rid of the cancer, but we will focus on comfort. Hospice strives to treat pain and anxiety, and focus on getting favorite meals, and similar comforts for the patient in the time they have left.

The intensity of the ICU makes for a very reduced quality of life for the patient. **Even if it could extend life by a few days with more IV fluids, X rays, tests, multiple exams by nurses and doctors and even surgery, the ICU may not be**

the place we would want our loved ones to spend their last days. Hospice provides a means for the patient to be with family. It is focused on comfort and making sure the patient isn't in pain. Additionally, hospice provides support for the families and allows them to be much closer to the patient as they don't have the strict hospital visitation rules.

A Case Manager or a Social Worker usually helps the team set up Hospice Care. Let your ICU Nurse know if you are interested in talking with Hospice, they can always come and talk with you. If it is a good fit for you and your family, you will know and you will feel right about making the transition. If it doesn't seem the right fit for your situation, you will have a sense of that as well.

15). What is Brain Death?

This is a very confusing term that is often used in the ICU, one I wish we had never started using. When someone has a Catastrophic Brain Insult (such as a gunshot to the head, a massive stroke or a cardiac arrest with no oxygen to the brain for a prolonged period of time or a serious brain infection, etc.), it is not uncommon for the patient to make it to the ICU and be put on Life Support. Life Support will help them breathe (provide oxygen) and Support their heart, etc. And if we didn't know that the brain is in such a critical state, it could seem that the patient is now doing relatively OK.

Sadly, because the BIG PICTURE is that the brain has been seriously injured, it can be the case that the patient's brain function continues to decline (based on the neurological exam or the swelling visible in the brain pictures) and the brain no longer shows signs of life. This is a big deal because it is the brain that tells our bodies that we have to breathe and that breath is what brings oxygen for the heart to continue to pump blood to all the organs. It is our brain that is the "Command Center" for all of our organs. **Truly, once the brain is gone, though machines can mechanically cause certain functions to continue, that person is no longer alive.**

When we suspect that this is the case, we carry out specific neurological exams, check that the patient is not on any medications such as morphine that can make them "sleepy", and make sure that nothing else explains this picture. After carefully evaluating each of these areas, we carry out an exam to check for signs of brain activity. Next we have to perform a Perfusion Scan (a confirmatory test to check for any blood flow to the brain) or an Apnea Test (to see if the patient will start breathing on their own). These tests will CONFIRM the clinical suspicion that the brain is no longer functioning. When these have been confirmed, we know the patient has passed away.

Confusion can sometimes set in at this point. Sometimes we communicate that the patient is "Brain dead" but the family can still see the heart beating and the Ventilator working and they think the patient is still alive and that only the brain is dead. **It is key that families understand that a Brain death determination is the same as a pronouncement of death. Unfortunately, this determination is final and the patient now needs to be disconnected from the machines.**

This situation is not to be confused with a Prolonged Coma from which some patients have been known to wake up after years. Patients in a Prolonged Coma have some brain activity on their neurological exam, so there can't be a determination of Brain Death. A Brain Death evaluation is only carried out when there are no signs of brain activity during the various exams that are done following a catastrophic event to the brain.

Brain Death is one of the hardest issues to deal with, and it is critical for the Medical Team to communicate closely with the family, keeping them posted during all the steps of this evaluation so that they understand, and are prepared for, the outcome.

After the Brain death determination, it is common that representatives from Organ Donor Organizations approach the family to have a conversation. Some patients in this situation are already registered as Organ Donors but, if that's not the case, the family can still choose to donate the patient's organs and provide the gift of life to other patients that are waiting for an organ to continue living.

CHAPTER 8

Questions to Ask the ICU Team

A quick reference for "Good Questions" to ask

This chapter is intended to help you be prepared to ask questions when talking to the Medical Team.

REMEMBER what is important to have clear:

A. What is the BIG PICTURE, the main problem that is making your loved one sick? Is this because of an infection? Is this because of a failing organ? (heart, lungs, brain,etc)

B. How is your loved one **responding to treatment**?

C. Are there **complications** to worry about?

If you don't have these 3 points clear, your conversation should focus on getting clarity on these three points.

1). How is (insert patient's name) doing today?

Look for Better/ the same/ worse. Ask for clarification if they use the word "Stable."

2). What are the goals for today?

3). Are there new things to worry about?

4). For Intubated/on Vent patients:

- Is the reason the patient was put on the Vent (Pneumonia, Heart Failure, Sepsis, etc) getting better?

- Is the Ventilator doing less for the patient? (This is a good thing, and means the patient is breathing more on their own.)

- Is the patient waking up OK or are they agitated when the sedation is decreased? This is very important. If the patient is agitated (a condition we call Delirium), even if the lungs heal, this will delay the removal of the Breathing Tube.

- How close are we to trying to see if the patient can breathe on his own?

5). For Comatose/Unresponsive patients:

- Is there any improvement today? Is the patient more responsive? *(A caution about interpreting the patient "squeezing" your hand. Even the sickest patients will do this as a reflex and not intentionally.)*

- Trust what you see: is the patient opening their eyes? Do they make eye contact? Do they track you when you move?

- Is the reason for this (stroke, drug toxicity, infection) getting better?

- If there was a Catastrophic Event to the brain, are there concerns for deterioration and potential loss of brain function? Any concerns for swelling in the brain?

6). For Septic patients:

- Sometimes the sickest patients with Sepsis (an extreme response to an infection that spreads throughout the body) need medication to keep the Blood Pressure up and out of Septic Shock. Is this getting better?

- Are Antibiotics working, is the infection clearing?

- Are there other organs failing due to the Sepsis? How are they doing? Is there confusion (a sign of brain failure), Kidney Failure, is the heart affected, is the liver inflamed?

7). For Heart Failure patients:

More people die from heart problems than any other cause, a lot of people live with weak hearts that can be "compensated" until something happens and makes the heart fail.

- What caused the heart to fail? Is this something that can be fixed? (as in a Heart Attack) or is this chronic? (As in the case of someone who has had multiple Heart Attacks or has a stiff heart from years with Blood Pressure issues.)

- Is the heart able to pump the blood to the other organs or are they failing because it cannot?

- Does this have a solution? Does the patient qualify for advanced forms of Life Support like a Left Ventricular Assist Device (an implanted pump that can be used for a while) or even a Heart Transplant?

- If it is temporary, will ECMO help? Can it be explored as an option even if it means transfering the patient to an ECMO hospital?

8). For Kidney Failure patients:

- Is this a new problem that can reverse with time or did the patient already have sick kidneys? (This could make it harder for the patient to overcome the illness.)

- Are the kidneys getting better or worse?

- Is the patient making urine?

- IF on Dialysis: is the patient tolerating the Dialysis OK?

9). For patients with infections: (*These questions are similar to the Sepsis questions, as Sepsis comes from an infection but is an exaggerated response.*)

- Do they know the source of the infection? (Common places are the urine, the lungs, skin infections, and sometimes the abdomen.)

- Are Antibiotics working? Is the bacteria covered by the Antibiotics being used?

- Is there need for "source control", like removing an infected collection or draining an infected gallbladder?

- Did they repeat the cultures and do they look better now?

- Is the infection in the blood?

10). For patients with a failing Liver (Liver Cirrhosis)

Sadly, the amount of support that can be provided to patients with Liver Failure is very limited. There is no equipment that can do the work of the liver, as opposed to Hemodialysis Machines (that help the kidneys), Ventilators (that help the lungs) or machines/medications that can help the heart. Even with the help of a Liver Specialist (Hepatologist) these patients can be the sickest patients in the ICU.

A failing liver is usually the result of years of problems (usually alcoholism or Hepatitis or both) and when the patients get sick to the point of coming to the ICU, they are very sick.

It is very rare that a healthy liver fails, and it is usually due to an Acetaminophen overdose or other drug toxicities. In extremely rare cases it can be caused by severe blood clotting.

The most important question here is:

- Can this liver heal? The reason this is important is because we can't live without a liver and there are no machines that support its function. **The only solution is getting a new liver with a liver transplant. To give someone a transplant is a very complicated process and it can take weeks before a team can do a complete evaluation.** This evaluation involves the patient's health but also has to take into consideration how much support the patient has from family. Most of the time, an urgent transplant is simply not an option for an ICU patient. In Liver Cirrhosis, healthy liver cells are replaced with scarred tissue that has no ability to heal. This basically means that the liver has failed.

The doctors can tell by evaluating the patient whether the liver is in bad shape or not. They use a combination of exam findings and lab values to calculate how badly damaged the liver is and how this will impact the patient (it is called a MELD Score). Sadly, patients with a bad liver go in and out of the hospital with complication after complication and the Predicted Mortality (the chance that they will die) can be very high.

These patients tend to be very weak (they lose a lot of muscle mass), they get confused very quickly and are typically dependent on others. When they get to this point and they are going in and out of the hospital, recovery is almost impossible.

While it is fair to give these patients a chance, if they are not candidates for a transplant, their options are limited. At this point the question, "What are our goals now?" becomes very important.

Questions to ask about a patient with a bad liver:

- How bad was the liver before the patient got sick enough to come to the ICU? If the answer is that the patient had "advanced" or bad Cirrhosis, this is very serious since this liver cannot repair itself.

- What made the patient get sick this time?

  This is usually caused by an infection, a bleeding episode or a toxin build up. The key is to try to reverse this and see if the liver can recover some of its function.

- Do you have signs that the liver is getting better?

  The answer to this is a combination of things:

  a. In the physical exam, the patient may wake up and show signs of strength.

  b. Some lab numbers may get better.

  c. If the patient was bleeding, the bleeding stops.

  d. The other organs don't fail.

- How are the kidneys doing?

  There is an important "connection" between a failing liver and how patients do when the kidneys fail. If the team was able to act quickly when the patient arrived in the ICU and the patient still had the ability to recover, this is good news as long as the kidneys aren't affected. If the kidneys fail, typically the prognosis is much worse.

- Can the patient get a new liver?

That is a fair question to ask. In rare cases, an emergency liver transplant can be done, however, the answer most likely will be "No". In the first place, this is because the evaluation is complex and is very rarely begun once the patient is in the ICU, but also because the patient needs to be strong enough to survive the surgery. Sometimes patients on the Transplant Waiting List come to the ICU sick and need to be cared for until they get strong enough to hopefully survive the Transplant Surgery (in the event that a matching liver becomes available). Deciding when a patient is ready to go to Transplant Surgery can be a very difficult decision.

11) For patients recovering from Surgery:

- How is the recovery from surgery going? Is everything as expected?

- If the patient has tubes/drains: are they having the expected drainage?

- Does the wound look ok?

- Are there any complications to be worried about?

CHAPTER 9

I wrote this book to help you walk through your ICU experience. The ICU can be an intimidating environment for those that aren't used to it. Even some doctors that don't work in the ICU are intimidated by its pace and stress level, so don't feel badly if this was the case with you at the beginning.

Remember, feeling you can trust the ICU Team to do what is best for your loved one is vital as it partners with you and your loved one's family to deliver the best care possible.

The pandemic days where the families were removed from the ICU truly exposed the essential nature of this lost relationship. Families suffered separation, loss and fear of the unknown. The ICU Team members became exhausted and dealt with grief and rejection. It is my hope that this book will aid in restoring the critical bond between the ICU Team and the family and allow them to work together to provide the best care possible for the ICU patient.

GLOSSARY OF TERMS

A

Appendicitis 15
Arterial Line 8, 68

B

Balloon Pump 7, 21, 53, 61
BIG PICTURE 39, 44, 45, 46, 80, 83, 86, 92, 93, 96, 102, 106, 109
Brain Death 106, 108
Bronchoscopy 8, 70

C

Cardiothoracic ICU 32
Cardioversion 8, 72
Case Manager 7, 35, 51, 87, 103, 106
Central Line 8, 67, 68
Chaplain 7, 36
Chest Tube 8, 70
Cirrhosis 114, 115, 116
Closed ICU 28
Code Blue 98
Code Status 8
Comatose 9, 110
CPR 9, 95, 97, 98, 100, 101
Critical Period 7, 40, 45
CRRT 60, 61

D

Decision Maker 35, 103
Device 7, 21, 53, 61, 112
Dialysis Machine 7, 53, 60
Dietician 7, 34
Discharge 8, 35, 52, 87, 88

DNI 97
DNR 97
Drainage 8, 73

E

ECMO 1, 7, 20, 22, 25, 53, 62, 63, 88, 112
End of Life 9, 93, 94, 95, 100
Exit Plan Period 40, 50

F

Family Member 2, 3, 42, 49, 51, 56, 77, 80, 81, 82, 101, 104
Feeding Tube 8, 17, 51, 66, 87, 90
Fellow 32, 76
Foley Catheter 8, 65, 66
Full Code 96

H

Heal 18, 23, 24, 39, 46, 54, 58, 72, 95, 101, 102, 110, 114, 115
Heart Failure 9, 71, 110, 112
Hemodialysis Catheter 8, 68
Hospice 9, 105, 106
Housekeepers 36

I

ICU Attending 31, 32
ICU Checklist 46
ICU Equipment 54, 88
ICU Monitor 53, 55
ICU Nurse 1, 2, 29, 30, 31, 42, 45, 46, 60, 75, 106
ICU Pharmacist 7
ICU Team 8, 11, 16, 17, 19, 22, 26, 29, 32, 35, 37, 40, 41, 42, 43, 44,
        46, 47, 49, 56, 60, 61, 62, 65, 68, 76, 78, 79, 80, 81, 82, 83,
        85, 86, 87, 92, 93, 95, 98, 102, 103, 119
Impella Device 7, 53, 61
Infections 9, 72
Infusion Pump 7, 53, 56, 57, 66, 88
Intern 2, 3, 32, 67, 82
Intubation 8, 69

K

Keep Going 9, 101
Kidney Failure 9, 112

L

Liver Failure 114

M

Medical ICU 76
Medical Power of Attorney 43, 103
Medication 21
Monitoring 21, 22, 55

N

Neurosurgical ICU 19, 28, 32
No Escalation of Care 97
Nurse Practitioner 32
Nutritionist 34

P

Paracentesis 8, 72
Patient Portal 83
Pediatric ICU 28
PEG Tube 90
Physical Therapy 16, 77

R

Recovery and Waiting Period 40, 45
Rehabilitation 8, 16, 35, 91
Resident 32, 76, 104
Respiratory Therapists 7, 33, 79

S

Septic 9, 111
Social Worker 7, 35, 87, 106
Surgery 9, 20, 117
Surgical ICU 19, 28, 32